If you have enjoyed *Travels with my Zebra*, you might like to try David Lawrence's other books and booklets for young people:

The Chocolate Teapot
surviving at school
(Scripture Union)

The Superglue Sandwich
for people who are stuck for an answer
(Scripture Union)

Home but not Alone
a guide to surviving hassles at home
(Marshall Pickering)

On Line with God
practical help with how to pray
(Scripture Union)

Big Questions about God and You
ideal booklet for 'interested' friends
(Scripture Union)

Help! My Parents are Aliens
booklet offering more help for coping at home
(Scripture Union)

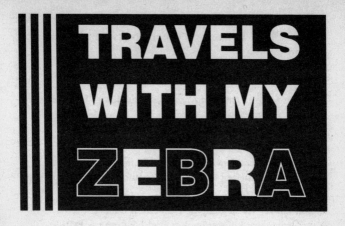

TRAVELS WITH MY ZEBRA

**Making choices when everything is
not black or white**

DAVID LAWRENCE

Scripture Union

© David Lawrence 1999
First published 1999
Scripture Union, 207–209 Queensway, Bletchley,
Milton Keynes, MK2 2EB, England

ISBN 1 85999 262 5

British Library Cataloguing-in-Publication Data.
A catalogue record of this book is available from the British
Library.

Printed and bound in Great Britain by Cox & Wyman Ltd,
Reading.

Acknowledgements

I would like to acknowledge the help of the following
people during the writing of this book:

My family Myrtle, Mark, Andrew and Tim who
encouraged me by laughing in the right places when
they read the manuscript.

Ro Willoughby at Scripture Union, and my editor,
Jenny Hyatt, who has patiently nursed me through
several bouts of writer's block.

Eric Morecambe, Spike Milligan, John Cleese and
Anthony Buckeridge who have made me laugh.

Christ the Rock Christian Fellowship, who gave me
time off to write.

Nancy Beard, who maintained my caffeine levels.

David Ormsby-Rymer, the ultimate Mr Fix-It, who
gave first aid to my computer when it suffered sudden
amnesia at the end of chapter four.

Introduction

In case you hadn't noticed, this book is in two parts.

The first part is a story about some homework of mine that went disastrously wrong. I can't tell you much more than that about it or I'll spoil it for you, but perhaps I should warn you that everyone who has read it so far has burst out into fits of laughter at frequent intervals. I strongly advise you therefore not to read it in the company of friends or else, each time you laugh, they'll keep asking, 'Now what's funny?', which is a real pain.

Throughout the story, the characters face some tough choices about what to do, how to behave, what to buy, what to watch... all the usual stuff, and at the end of each chapter there is a page highlighting the issues that have been raised in the story (just in case you missed them while you were laughing).

The last bit of the book (starting on page 84) then looks at each issue in turn, helping you think through the choices that you will make when you next come face to face with that particular decision. (You don't have to read all of the 'CHOICES' pages because each one is complete in itself, so just turn to the ones that you're interested in at present and keep the book handy to turn to the others at a later date.)

Contents

Choices contents

Chapter 1

It was probably James Harris who made the biggest crash, although there was considerable debate about it afterwards.

What was beyond doubt was that Kevin Kavinsky had been the first to go, slumping to the ground and taking two other innocent bystanders with him. Kevin had been followed by Sophie Brophy, whose ballet training was widely held responsible for the way in which she managed to faint and slide gracefully under the table without a sound. In stark contrast to Sophie's dainty demise, Tim Framley keeled over with a loud moan, knocked two stools flying and hit his head on the floor with a sickening thump.

James Harris was probably about thirteenth on the list, and by then things were completely out of hand. But his *was* definitely the biggest crash.

I've always liked science lessons but I'd never imagined that they could get as exciting as this!

During the term we'd already done Chemistry (Question: 'What happens if you place a test tube of magnesium filings over a bunsen burner?' Answer: 'Nothing at all unless you light the bunsen.'), and the second module had been Physics.

Physics was in the second half-term and the experiments had the potential for a lot of fun if only Mr Grimshaw, our science teacher, didn't always stop things just as they reached the good bits.

For example, last term Mr Grimshaw had asked us to devise an experiment to test the relative strengths of two sets of batteries. Each set of batteries was to be joined together in different ways and then connected to some sort of device which they would have to power. The test was to see which way of joining up the batteries produced most power, and which way made the batteries last longest.

I was working with my mate, Kevin Kavinsky, and we had the brilliant idea of wiring up the batteries to his sister's hamster-wheel. The hamster (called Gertrude) was getting on a bit and Kev reckoned that the extra battery power would help her poor old legs keep the wheel turning in her daily exercise slot – once we'd sorted out which battery set-up worked best.

Gertrude plus wheel were duly smuggled into school on the day of the Physics experiment and while Mr Grimshaw was watching other people doing their experiment, we set up ours. We connected the batteries to a small electric motor (nicked from the Mini Cooper in my little brother's Scalextric), and joined the electric motor to the hamster-wheel.

Gertrude was placed inside the wheel and the final connection of battery to motor was made. The look on her face was of mild but pleasant surprise as the battery-assisted wheel slowly turned with very little effort from her ageing arthritic limbs. She almost grinned, in a hamsterish sort of way, as she glided effortlessly along, cheerily going nowhere within her gently spinning wheel.

'OK,' said Kev, 'that seems to work. Let's check to see if using the batteries the other way makes any difference.'

We probably should have thought, but we didn't. After all, it was an experiment, and some things you only find out by trial and error. We performed the error and Gertrude was to experience the trial!

As we connected the new set-up of batteries to the wheel (at the bottom of which Gertrude had now fallen asleep), the small motor made a high-pitched whining noise and started to turn at a terrific rate. The wheel span at six times its previous speed and the effect on Gertrude was alarming. She awoke to find herself tumbling out of control, performing 360-degree loop-the-loops inside her wheel, but as we watched, spellbound by this unexpected turn of events (if you'll pardon the pun), she somehow managed to regain her footing, and with eyes bulging and whiskers taut, she valiantly kept pace with the frantically spinning wheel.

Her efforts were worthy of an Olympic gold medal, but at this point Mr Grimshaw arrived, and he didn't seem to be in the mood for handing out prizes.

'What... I don't believe... I've never... I... I...'

Temporarily rendered verbally incoherent by the sight of Gertrude's sprinting ability, he nevertheless managed to do what we should have done had we not been so awestruck by the outcome of our experiment. He grabbed the wires joining the batteries to the motor and wrenched them apart, causing the wheel to slow immediately.

As Gertrude's sprint moderated to become first a jog and then a gentle walking pace, her breathing gradually returned to normal. She shook her head, twitched her whiskers, looked up at us with a proud sort of 'And-you-thought-I-was-past-it' look, before once again nestling down to sleep in the base of the now-motionless wheel.

If only Mr Grimshaw had suddenly been overcome with a similar desire to lie down and sleep, we would have been OK. But his red hair began to bob alarmingly as his head nodded vigorously. This was not good news, since Mr Grimshaw's famous 'nodding' was a well-known sign that he was very upset about something – and in this case the something seemed to be Kev and me.

(*Nod*) 'What on *earth* do you think you were doing?'

I attempted a reply. 'Well, sir...'

(*Nod*) 'Silence! Who asked you to speak?'

'We-e-ll, you did, si...'

(*Violent Nod* – bad sign.) '**Silence**! This is the most (*Nod*) disgraceful, (*Nod*) dangerous, (*Nod*) immature behaviour I've seen in my whole career. (*Nod*) Go and stand outside my office. I'll (*Nod*) sort you out later.'

See what I mean? Just as science experiments begin to get interesting, Mr Grimshaw steps in and stops them.

Anyway, I digress. Back to Friday morning's lesson. Having mastered Chemistry and Physics, we were now on to Biology. We'd spent weeks doing plants and stuff (how many petals on a buttercup – and who cares anyway?) and now we were on to 'The Human Body' and about to get into eyes. Literally.

Mr Grimshaw had not prepared us adequately, we felt. If a film had been made of the things he was about to do in our lesson, it would have had an '18' rating and been placed on the very top shelf of the local video rental store.

In the name of science, Mr Grimshaw had produced an Eye (not one of his own, you understand, and not one that anyone was still in need of), but nevertheless, there looking at us from the dissecting dish on his demonstration bench was an Eye.

My mind raced to explore the implications of this bizarre stunt. I wondered, as I looked at it, what had been the last thing that it had seen before being plucked from its socket. Who had its last owner been and, darkest thought of all, who did Mr Grimshaw know who could supply spare body parts to school science teachers?

For goodness' sake, this was only Year 9! If an *eye* was produced for us at our tender age, whatever took place in the secret darkness behind the blinds in Year 10 and 11 science lessons? And what if you took science subjects at A-level? Perhaps the rumours that the creepy Mr Strang, the French teacher, was made up of spare parts were actually true. Maybe he was the unhappy result of an A-level failures 'Body Part Recycling' project.

As we sat there, strangely mesmerised by the unblinking stare of the Eye which Mr Grimshaw had placed in front of us, he began to speak.

'Now, who can remember from last lesson what we call the various parts of the eye?'

He looked around for a response, but no one felt able to speak. It occurred to me that perhaps, unwittingly, Mr Grimshaw had stumbled upon the perfect answer to unruly classes. That eye had even the most boisterous of our class members mute with silent admiration (or sheer terror); even James Harris hadn't spoken for several minutes. Maybe if all teachers had a range of dismembered limbs and body organs in their desk drawers, they would only have to whip them out to restore order to even the most difficult of their classes. I was just wondering which teacher might choose which internal organ as their preferred means of discipline when I was aware that Mr Grimshaw was moving into action.

'Very well then,' he said, 'seeing as we all seem to have lost our tongues' (a singularly poor choice of phrase in the circumstances, I thought), 'we had better have a look inside this eye, to see if we can refresh our memories.'

In all honesty, I could not bring myself to believe that looking inside the eye would refresh anything very much. And what is more, I could not bring myself to believe that Mr Grimshaw, that most sensible and ordinary of teachers, could bring himself to plunge the scalpel that he was brandishing, into the eye. After all, he drove a Ford Escort and wore Clarks shoes; surely such a man would not be capable of such barbarity.

Just then, something my mum said came back to my mind. It was after our seemingly docile spaniel had come in one morning with a mouthful of postman's trousers. Mum looked at her, shook her head and said, 'Well, well. I never thought you had it in you, but they do say it's always the quiet ones.'

'Always the quiet ones.' Hmm. I looked at Mr Grimshaw and was beginning to wonder what other excesses this mild-mannered man was capable of, when he took the scalpel and made an incision around the side of the eye. Ignoring the inky black fluid that squirted out and formed a small puddle on his desk, he put his fingers into the slit he had created, gently pulled open the eye and held it up for our inspection.

His tone was matter of fact. 'All right then, look in there. *Now* can anyone remember the name of any parts of the eye?'

We never found out because it was at this point that Kevin Kavinsky collapsed and started an avalanche of bodies that made the very floor of the classroom shake. Out of thirty-one in the class that day, only twelve were left standing (and eleven of those had their eyes so tightly closed that it was halfway through the following break before they could see clearly again.

The only one who was unaffected by the spectacle (or should that be monocle?) was Alex Britton whose dad owned the butcher's shop down the High Street. His dad often brought home the odd animal carcass to hack to bits in the family kitchen, so Alex had become hardened to the sight of raw flesh being cut up under his very nose. (Incidentally, one unforeseen bonus of the whole episode for Alex was that he became the grateful recipient of fifteen unwanted packed lunches that day.)

Anyway, as you can imagine, the lesson had disintegrated into chaos. Mr Grimshaw abandoned any hope of leading a meaningful investigative science lesson and spent what time remained trying to revive and bandage the worst casualties.

In the middle of it all he rather rashly tried to set homework, but everyone was in such an emotionally fragile state that no one heard what he said – a failure of communication which was to produce unexpected results.

No, but seriously...

'Gertrude awoke to find herself tumbling out of control...'

This book is about making choices. Sometimes (as Gertrude discovered in her wheel), other people can make choices which can turn *our* world upside down. For example, if your parents decide to move house, your teachers decide to give your class a detention or the government decides to ban school (dream on), your world would be affected no matter what you might think about it.

But you can't always blame other people for what goes on in your life. Every week you make hundreds of decisions which affect your life, and the scary thing is that most of them you don't even stop to think about!

Where to go, who to go with, what to spend, what to watch, what to tell your parents, how to cope with your little brother... and on and on. Choices, choices, choices.

But how do you decide? What makes you choose one thing over another – and does it really matter anyway?

If you want to take a minute to chew over how to make sound choices, turn to page 85.

If not, read on...

Chapter 2

By the end of the afternoon session most of the class had recovered. The only remaining casualty was Alex Britton who had felt more sick the longer the afternoon had gone on. In fact, by the last lesson (Music with Miss Pugh), he had to ask to be excused. He raised his hand and when Miss Pugh's raised eyebrow signalled permission to speak, he said,

'Please, Miss, can I leave the room?'

Not unreasonably, Miss Pugh asked, 'Why?'

'Because I don't feel well, Miss.'

Now no teacher worthy of the name will take that one at face value, so the inevitable supplementary question followed.

'What sort of "not well"?'

There was no point in beating about the bush, so Alex confessed, 'I think I'm going to be horribly sick, Miss.'

Any normal human being would immediately evacuate to a discreet distance someone who claimed to be about to vomit violently. But not a teacher. They are trained to stand fast in the face of such danger, and Miss Pugh was not about to dismiss Alex on the basis of such an unsubstantiated claim. More information was needed before anyone could escape her lesson. After all, imagine the terminal damage done to a child's educational development if they were to miss even five minutes of her scintillating demonstration of the manufacture of oboe reeds, just to be sick. She decided to investigate.

'You must have eaten something that didn't agree with you at lunchtime. What did you have?'

Something deep inside Alex began to move and he decided that he did not have the stomach (so to speak) to list all the contents of the fifteen packed lunches that he had consumed. He tried a pleading tone.

'Do I *have* to tell you, Miss?'

Miss Pugh, sensing that Alex was playing for time but misinterpreting the reason, countered with, 'Yes, you do. I'd like to know everything you ate which might have made you feel unwell.'

Alex, his stomach continuing to give warning signs of imminent eruption, decided that if the only way to get out of this room was to list what he had eaten, he would have a go but he would keep it simple and avoid unnecessary detail.

'OK, Miss. I had sandwiches, pies, cakes and drinks.'

Unfortunately for Alex, rather than satisfying Miss Pugh's thirst for information, this abbreviated version of his lunchtime marathon merely served to stimulate it even more.

'Well, that all sounds quite normal. I can't believe that you need to leave the room after such a straightforward lunch. What was in the sandwiches and pies?'

Alex, now getting desperate, gripped the sides of his desk and began to list what he could remember of his lunch.

'OK, Miss, as far as I can remember the sandwiches were cheese and pickle, fish paste, beef paste, ham and lettuce, peanut butter and marmalade, marmite, tuna and salad cream, and some other stuff...'(*pause to regain*

19

control of his quivering insides while Miss Pugh stared incredulously) '... and the pies were pork, chicken and mushroom, apple and blackcurrant, ham and pickle, apricot...'

At this point he stopped again, not because of anything Miss Pugh had said but because the very mention of the ham and pickle pies from Tom Reynolds' lunch had started the contents of his stomach on an unstoppable upward journey. The time for gaining permission was past and the time for taking action had arrived. Alex leapt to his feet and was last seen clutching the wastepaper bin to his face, running down the corridor towards the boys' loos.

He still had not reappeared by the end of the lesson and his dramatic disappearance, together with

reflections on the incident of Mr Grimshaw's Eye, formed the major topic of conversation on the bus as we travelled home. As usual, things got more exaggerated with each retelling and, depending on who was speaking, the heroes and villains changed places. So when Mark Todd (Toddy) was speaking, it was *he* who had been the last to fall under the influence of the Eye and he had only fallen then because Garry Bone (Gazza) had fallen first and knocked him for six on the way down. However, to hear Gazza speak, you would have thought that *he* had remained composed to the last and, far from falling in a faint, had decided to sit down on the floor in protest at the barbarity of what Mr Grimshaw was doing.

As I got off at my bus stop, I left them all still arguing about whose nerve had held longest and about how Alex had managed to dispose of the contents of Miss Pugh's rubbish bin.

Our house was only a couple of minutes' walk from the bus stop. It was on one of those modern estates where the houses all look the same, or at least they did when they were built. In the intervening years these identical brick boxes had acquired personalities of their own, as each resident shaped their home according to their own interests and ambitions.

Number 3 was Mr and Mrs Brown. Mr Brown was heavily into DIY car repairs and his front lawn was always strewn with the dismembered carcasses of several old cars which had been cannibalised to repair Mr Brown's own pride and joy, a 1973 Ford Capri.

Number 5 was Mrs Arbottle. Mrs Arbottle had a longing to live in a country cottage but could only afford to live in a house on our estate. She tried to compensate by training roses up the side of her house, installing 'lattice-look' double glazing and calling her house 'Willow Tree Cottage'. To be frank, it just looked ridiculous.

And so it went on until I arrived at Number 24, our house. It was a pity that my dad was a Country and Western freak, for all sorts of reasons, but the one that caused me most public humiliation was the way that he had hired a professional sign-writer to paint a five-foot-high picture of Dolly Parton on a Stars and Stripes background on our garage door. Admittedly it meant that no one ever got lost trying to find our house, but apart from that it was nudging ten out of ten on the scale of 'Cringeworthy Things To Do To The Outside Of Your House'. But that was my dad for you. He, like all dads, was the final authority on all things and was never shy about letting the world in general (and me in particular) have the benefit of his superior knowledge.

Dad knew all about everything, but his specialist subjects were Music, Fashion, Financial Planning and History. Such was his grasp of these subjects that he could sometimes lecture on all four at once. Just recently, for example, he wandered into my bedroom one evening as I was getting ready to go out with my mates. As usual I was listening to one of my grungy CDs as I applied the last 'tsssst' of Sphynx Amazonia to my socks.

Dad opened up with a question. 'What are you doing with that aerosol? That stuff's supposed to go under your arms, not on your clothes.'

I was in a hurry. 'Dad, don't start. I paid for it and I can put it where I like.'

Dad was not in a hurry. 'There's no need to take that tone, I was only making an observation. I know you paid for it, and I dare say you paid a fortune, didn't you?

How much did it cost? A pound? One-fifty?'

Since he never bought his own deodorant, Dad had no idea. Without thinking, I put him right. 'A *pound*? Dad, you're so out of touch. This stuff costs £3.45 a can.'

As soon as I had said it, I knew I'd fallen into his trap and laid out the red carpet for a right royal lecture.

'*Three pounds forty-five*? You must want your brains tested. When I was a lad, me and my mates used to collect rose petals in jam jars, and crush them in water to make our own aftershave. Didn't cost a penny and if you were careful it lasted for months. Now you youngsters seem to think that money grows on trees and think nothing of buying smelly stuff to rot your socks at three pounds forty-five a tin.' (Dad never used the term 'can' which, garage door notwithstanding, he considered a crude Americanism.)

He was warming to his task and I knew there was nothing I could say to stop him. Quite the contrary. Any further comment from me would merely fuel his ranting. Even without my assistance, he went on anyway:

'And what's this row coming out of your hi-fi? Is this record on the right speed?' (CDs, like 'cans', were from a universe several light years removed from Dad's.) 'If that guy's a guitarist, I'm a tin of corned beef. And listen to that awful moaning sound. Does she call that singing? You can't even hear the words. Now if you listen to one of my Dolly Parton discs, you can hear every word she says. Clear as a bell and twice as beautiful.'

My life was slipping away from me so I tried to bring our encounter to an end. 'Dad, the day I listen to one of your Dolly Parton records is the day grass turns purple, fish fly and you acquire some fashion sense. Now I'm going out. Goodbye.'

I thought that was quite witty (and not a little cutting) but, far from terminating Dad's concise lecture series, this merely introduced his final specialism. Fashion. It never ceased to amaze me that someone who could wear tank tops, floral ties and checked caps (and on a bad day wear them all at the same time) could dare to lecture me on fashion. But he did.

'Not dressed like that you're not.'

I let out a warning 'Daaad!', but to no avail.

'Haven't you got a decent pair of jeans to wear? Those are all faded. And look at the state of your hair. You could at least dry it before you go out.'

With frustration rising I answered back, 'Dad, I bought these jeans precisely *because* they looked faded and I've got wet-look gel on my hair so it's *supposed* to look wet. Surely even *you* can work that one out. Now will you please get out of my way because I'm late.'

I pushed past Dad who was muttering, 'Wet-look gel. What on earth is wet-look gel?', and made my way outside.

Anyway, that was my dad for you. But as I went indoors today it was my mum who greeted me.

'Hello, have a nice a day at school, dear?'

She always asked that. It was a silly question since no one ever had a nice day at school. Schools were just not created for having nice days in. They were created with the sole purpose of giving you a hard time and teaching you what you cannot do, so that when you do the things you like to do *outside* school, you suddenly feel good about yourself. However, Mum deserved an answer so I gave her one.

'Nothing special. Usual sort of stuff. Mr Grimshaw

stuck a knife in an eye and Alex Britton was sick in Miss Pugh's bin.'

Mum's attention was momentarily drawn away from the TV chat show she was watching.

'Oh, poor lad. I'm not surprised he was sick, it must have hurt like anything. Why did Mr Grimshaw do it? Was Alex being naughty?'

'He didn't stick the knife in *Alex's* eye. Honestly Mum, what sort of school do you think you send me to every day?'

Mum, reassured that eye-piercing was not after all a permitted disciplinary technique at my school, resumed watching show host Jerry Spencer solve the previously terminal problems of the Smiths' failing marriage just in time for the adverts to start (neat how he always managed that). I drifted off to change, raid the biscuit tin and sneak out to play football before Mum could utter the dreadful words, 'Got any homework, love?'

With a mouthful of custard creams and wearing my old gear, I was about to sneak out of the back door when Mum's laser-guided hearing system locked onto the rustle of my tracksuit trousers.

'Got any homework, love?'

Drat, dratter, drattest. She got me again.

'I'm not sure, Mum. I'll just ring Kevin to find out.'

Mum now appeared in the kitchen from where my escape bid through the back door had been foiled.

'Whyever do you need to "ring Kevin to find out"? You've just spent all day with him at school and you've got ears the same as he has. What did your teachers say? Homework or no homework?'

I vaguely remembered Mr Grimshaw muttering something amid the chaos of the end of his lesson so I said, 'Well, I think we might have some Biology but I need to ask Kevin if he wrote it down because I was unconscious at the time.'

'Oh yes, and I'm the Queen of Sheba. All right, get on with it, but don't spend long on there. You know how your dad worries about the bill.'

As I rang Kevin I was silently praying that he'd be out, but no deal.

'Three-two-seven-seven-nine-twohoo. Kevin-speaking-and-who-are-youhoo?' (He always answered the phone like that. He was proud of it, as it was the only poem he'd ever written that actually rhymed.)

'Hi, Kevin. David here. Listen, I can't be long. My mum's breathing down my neck.'

'Oh, heavy. OK. What's up?'

'Nothing. Have we got any homework tonight? I kind of remember Mr Grimshaw saying something at the end of Biology but I wasn't quite with it at the time. Did you manage to write anything in your homework diary?'

I didn't think for one minute that Kev even knew where his homework diary was, but sadly I was wrong.

'Yeah,' he said. 'I wasn't feeling too good myself so I scribbled something down so I wouldn't forget. Hang on, I'll get it.'

I could hear the sound of his footsteps receding into the background and then approaching the phone again.

'Here it is. Wow. Hard to read or what! Umm, yeah, I've got it.' He spoke slowly as though deciphering a complicated code. 'Take... Body... Horse-like... Mammal. Yeah, that's it. Take body horse-like mammal.'

This sounded as though it was still in code, so I asked, 'What on earth does that mean? "Take body horse-like mammal".' Either Mr Grimshaw had flipped or Kevin had and to be honest, knowing them both, it was hard to choose which was the more likely. I asked for clarification.

'Well, what do you think he expects us to do?'

A pause as Kevin considered the mystical workings of Grimshaw's grey matter and then he offered, 'Well, I suppose he wants us to find a picture of a horse-like mammal and take it in for our next lesson. Maybe we've finished the human body course and we're moving on to horse-like bodies. I don't know, but it's a nice easy homework, eh? Shouldn't take more than a couple of minutes.'

That was true enough so, as I rang off, I turned to face Mum who was beating three eggs into submission before scrambling them in a saucepan (it could have been worse; they could have grown up and been spit-roasted).

'It's OK, Mum, we've only got to find a picture of a horse-type thing and take it in to show Mr Grimshaw. It won't take me a minute when I get in so can I go out now? Everyone will wonder where I've got to.'

Mum reluctantly agreed that I could go but as I went out I couldn't help but muse over our homework. 'Take body horse-like mammal'. Strange way of putting it, but then it was Mr Grimshaw.

No, but seriously...

'Dad knew all about everything...'

They always do! Living with parents presents you with all sorts of tough choices.

Whether to take any notice of what they say, or whether to do your own thing; whether to listen in silence or whether to answer back; whether to tell them the bare truth or whether to dress it up a bit; whether to accept their standards or whether to choose some of your own.

Tough choices! If you want some advice about coping with parents, turn to page 86.

* * * * * *

'I bought these jeans precisely *because* they looked faded...'

Choosing the right image is a *big* choice. What you listen to, what you wear — even what deodorant you choose — all say something about the sort of person you want to be known as.

But who is on hand to help you make this most mammoth set of choices? We are. Turn to page 87 for some input on image selection.

On the other hand, if you're not bothered, read on...

Chapter 3

I woke and looked at my Michael Owen bedside Alarm Clock and Pencil Sharpener (£8.99, but don't tell Dad). Half past seven. I groaned inwardly. I had discovered a cruel kind of genetic flaw in humanity which means that when you have to get up for school at half past seven, no amount of parental shaking and yelling can wake you up. But come Saturday, when you have the opportunity for a decent lie-in, you wake up at 7.30 sharp and can't get back to sleep however hard you try. In fact, the harder you try to empty your mind and drift back to sleep, the more you become locked into mental overdrive, wrestling with a stream of stimulating questions ranging from the mundane 'Where *did* I put the key to my bike-lock?' to the fantastic 'Who first milked a cow and what did he think he was doing at the time?'

Genetic flaws aside, however, the greatest obstacle to a Saturday snooze was my dad. During the week he is up and off to work before I fall out of bed, but at weekends it is different. On Saturdays he gets up at 7.30 and has a shower in the bathroom next to my bedroom. Now that in itself is not a problem, but what causes the upheaval is Dad's insistence on singing in the shower. He can't seem to help it, poor old chap. The minute that water starts flowing, Dad's voice starts bellowing. His voice is kind of operatic in a nasal kind of way – sort of

Pavarotti meets Donald Duck – and, boy, does he let rip.

The sheer volume is enough to raise the dead, never mind half-asleep sons in adjoining rooms. But what makes matters infinitely worse is that instead of singing recognisable songs, he makes up silly little ditties which he keeps repeating over and over and over and over again (and again!) until anyone within earshot is resigned to going insane or frantically phoning the travel agents for last-minute package holidays to anywhere at all as long as they leave *now*.

Today's Choral Classic was inspired by the sight of the new shampoo that Mum had bought, and it went to the tune of 'When the saints go marching in':

'Tesco shampoo
Is good for you,
It cleanses right down to the roots.
It leaves your hair so nice and shiny,
Just like that other stuff from Boots.'
(Repeat about 15 million times)

Anyway, today being a Saturday and with the usual (unwanted) help from Dad, I was wide awake by 7.45 and planning in my mind how to spend the day. All my best mates were out for the day with their families or grounded for bad behaviour, so I was all alone – a good excuse to drop in on Uncle Theo.

Uncle Theo forms the one-man lunatic fringe of our family. He is as different from my mum (his sister) as the proverbial chalk is from cheese. Mum is sensible, predictable and was definitely at the back of the queue when the sense of humour was being handed out. Uncle Theo on the other hand is loud, wild, loves practical jokes and has a laugh so hearty that once, after a particularly good joke, the neighbours had come around to complain that they couldn't hear their stereo and could he please stop his donkey braying!

You can see why I loved to visit Uncle Theo. I wouldn't dream of exposing my friends to his over-the-top personality but when, as today, I had the odd hour to kill on my own, I was always guaranteed a warm welcome and his place was a good bet for an interesting morning out.

Uncle Theo's 'place' was actually a flat above his shop and by the time I arrived, he had already made the trip downstairs from his living quarters to his place of work: 'Jock Theo's Emporium of Quality Used Goods'. (I should say that Jock wasn't his real name. His parents had called him Cecil, but Uncle Theo had taken such a dislike to his name that when as a teenager he had discovered that he had Scottish ancestors, he'd adopted the name Jock and had insisted on using it ever since.)

Ever since I was small I had loved to spend time in Uncle Theo's shop. It was basically a second-hand shop from which Uncle Theo sold (or tried to sell) as wide a range of oddments as you could imagine. Most of Uncle Theo's stock came from the houses of old people who had died with no relatives to take on their stuff. He moved in, bought the entire contents of their house and put them in his shop. The trouble was that far more people seemed to have died in the area than ever visited Uncle Theo's shop as customers. Consequently, his premises were bursting at the seams with just about any household item you could care to mention.

His stock was arranged in some sort of order so that as you walked down the narrow aisles, taking care to avoid the articles which were too large and which overflowed from their allotted place, you embarked on a journey of seemingly endless discovery.

On entering the door you were confronted by a large old bookcase filled with even older books, their covers faded and scuffed with age. Next to the bookcase, an upturned oil drum held an impressive array of sporting equipment: old wooden tennis and badminton racquets were crammed shoulder to shoulder with fishing rods, golf clubs, cricket bats and hockey sticks.

The oil drum stood next to the glass counter inside which Uncle Theo kept what he called 'my valuables'. In his 'valuables' collection today was an old car radio, an air pistol, a pre-historic computer and a gentleman's pocket watch inscribed on the back with the words 'Presented to Wilf Bartram 50 Glorious Years'. On the watch's front, a sticker bearing Uncle Theo's handwriting said: 'Valuable Watch. Spring broken but still right twice a day. Bargain £12.00'. That watch had been amongst Uncle Theo's 'valuables' for as long as I had been visiting his shop, so it seemed that none of his customers shared his opinion that paying £12.00 for a broken watch with an inscription to someone they had never heard of represented a 'bargain'!

As I entered the shop today, Uncle Theo was standing behind the glass counter serving a customer. He was dressed as usual in his kilt and a Braveheart sweatshirt which he had rescued from some stock that had been donated to his shop. He looked up as he heard the 'cling' of the doorbell and as he saw me his face widened into a broad smile.

'Davey, me lad. Capital! Capital to see you,' he boomed.

Everything was 'capital' to Uncle Theo. That was one of the reasons why I liked him so much.

He continued, 'Just give me a minute with this gentleman, and I'll be right with you. Have a look around. I've got some capital stuff in, ab-so-lutely capital!'

The invitation to look around the 'Emporium' was never one that I could refuse. I moved on from the glass 'valuables' counter, past a mountain of heavy wooden furniture, piled precariously high with the larger items like chests of drawers and wardrobes at the bottom and smaller ones like TV stands and piano stools perched right at the top, jammed against the ceiling.

Next was the 'Household Items' section. Shelf upon shelf of the most gaudy and unsightly pieces of china, glass and kitchenware. A teapot in the shape of a frog sat amid a pile of wooden spoons stained a hideous scarlet colour by their last job stirring I dreaded to think what. A set of glasses bearing the words 'Torremolinos 1973' sat beside a saucepan set with another of Uncle Theo's labels: 'Capital pan set, strong handles, non-stick (when made)'.

I don't know exactly what it is about Uncle Theo's Emporium but I could spend hours just looking at all of this junk. And, worse still, I could spend pounds and pounds that I haven't really got to spare on a lot of things that I am sure are such a bargain that I would be kicking myself forever if I were to miss out on them. Add to this the fact that Uncle Theo always gave me a 10% discount for being 'family', and you can understand why I seldom escaped from his shop without an armful of something or other which had proved irresistible.

In fact, the space under my cabin bed was almost full with stuff that had come from Uncle Theo's shop. Amongst my best bargain buys were some rusty garden shears with cracked wooden handles ('Be antique soon, me boy,' Uncle Theo had said. 'Capital investment'), a set of three wheels for a go-kart ('What if someone offers you a go-kart with only one wheel, me boy? You'll be laughing!'), and a stack of old LP records by people I'd never heard of like Bing Crosby and Max Bygraves ('Capitally collectable me boy. Cap-it-ally!').

I suppose I am not very different from just about anyone else really, because everyone I know has some kind of shop which they find totally addictive and from which they cannot escape without buying something – whether they need it or not.

For me it's Uncle Theo's Emporium which casts its spell, for Mum it's clothes shops and for most of my mates it's either the Diamond Discs music shop down at the mall or the local branch of Sportswise.

I remember the hoo-ha generated last year when I went with my mate Dixy (otherwise known as John Dixon) to buy some trainers from Sportswise. (I should tell you that my mum always warns me against hanging around with Dixy. 'Bad company corrupts good character,' she says whenever his name is mentioned. It is true that some of my closest brushes with the police have come in Dixy's company – an incident involving five on a bike attempting to break the land speed record down Watley's Hill comes to mind – but he's not that bad.)

Anyway, on the day in question, Dixy's mum had given him £35.00, which in her opinion was more than enough to get a 'nice comfortable pair of trainers', plus £30.00 for some shopping that Dixy was supposed to do on his way home.

The trouble is that Dixy's taste in footwear started at £50.00 and worked up, and as we stood in the shop and surveyed the possible options at £35.00, Dixy's heart sank.

'No way, Dave,' he exclaimed. 'There is no way I am going to be seen out wearing a pair of Sportswise own-brand trainers.'

I could see his point. Jason Bradstone had once turned up to school wearing just such a pair of trainers and took such a lot of stick that he 'accidentally' lost them out of the window of the top deck of the school bus. They may well be in Paris now, since as luck would have it, they fell onto the back of a passing lorry which carried the wording 'Geo. Davies. Express Carrier to Continental Europe'.

However, there seemed to be no answer to Dixy's dilemma since his mum had only given him £35.00 for shoes, so I decided that in order to hurry him up, I would try to talk him into buying something that he could afford, rather than spend the rest of the morning looking at stuff which he could not (and moaning all the time to me into the bargain).

'How about these? They're not too bad,' I suggested, as I pointed out a pair of £65 trainers reduced to £34.50 on the sale rack.

Dixy took a look. 'Better than those tacky Sportswise things, I suppose,' he said grudgingly. He took them down from the rack and had a closer look. It was about then that he got the idea which was to come so close to landing us in big trouble.

'Hey, Dave,' he whispered. 'I've got a brilliant idea.'

This seemed unlikely since Dixy had never been known to have a brilliant idea in his life. I was about to point this out when he continued anyway.

'You go over to the counter and talk to the assistant and I'll take this "SALE" sticker off these shoes and stick it on those Nike ones that I want.'

I was appalled. 'You can't do that!' I almost shouted.

'Shhh. Keep it down, you wally,' Dixy hissed. 'Come on. Everyone knows these shoes are overpriced anyway, so it won't really do any harm.'

I still don't know why I gave in, but I did. I sauntered innocently to the counter and engaged the young assistant in conversation about the relative merits of tinted and untinted swimming goggles while Dixy did the dastardly deed in the footwear department. As he approached the counter, he smiled at the young assistant.

'I'll take these please,' he said. 'Real bargain to get Nikes at that price.'

The shop assistant looked puzzled. 'Yes, it is.' He paused and took a closer look at the shoes and the 'SALE' sticker, as though trying to reassure himself of something before continuing, 'Real bargain, especially as these have only just come in.' Another pause, during which I was sure he could hear my heart thumping, before he said, 'Funny thing is, I bought a pair of these yesterday and I had to pay £65 for mine!'

Whoops! Dixy (to his credit) blushed. He began burbling. 'Crikey... Don't know how... the label said... but then... I thought it was too good to...' He ran out of steam under the unimpressed gaze of the assistant who, unbeknown to us, had this trick played on him on average about five times a week.

After a telling pause he spoke. 'Well, I can't let you have them at the "sale" price. Do you want them for their proper price, £65?'

Dixy, now so flustered that he would have sold his own knee caps to get out of that shop in one piece, said, 'Oh, yeah. Sure, that'll be fine,' before handing over the £35 which he had been given for shoes plus the extra £30 which was supposed to be for his mum's shopping.

(Since some people reading this book may be of a nervous disposition, I will not tell you what happened to Dixy when he got home and had to explain to his mum how he had 'lost' the £30 she'd given him for her stuff. It's enough to say that the story did not have a happy ending.)

Anyway, all that was just to show that whether it's trainers, clothes, CDs or – in my case – bargains from Uncle Theo's Emporium, the whole human race seems to be stuck with this curious addiction to want to spend money they haven't got, on things they don't really need for reasons that, when they get home and think about it, they cannot explain!

As I walked around Uncle Theo's shop that morning, I could almost feel this spending urge coming upon me. I stood for a little too long at the 'Electrical Appliances' section and was strangely attracted by an Arnold Schwarzenegger Electric Toothbrush before managing to wrench myself away and head towards my favourite section of the Emporium, Uncle Theo's 'Odds and Odder' department.

This was where Uncle Theo put all of the really strange things that he collected – the sorts of things that wouldn't happily fit into any of the other categories that he used for ordering the stock in his Emporium. It was tucked away at the back of the shop and as I made my way towards it, Uncle Theo joined me, his customer having departed happily clutching a pair of wellington boots (with sticker saying 'Guaranteed waterproof to depth of 2ft').

He put his arm around my shoulder, gave me a bone-bending hug, and said, 'Well now, Davey, me boy, this is an unexpected pleasure. What are you doing here today?'

I managed not to wince at the shrinkage which had occurred in my shoulder blades and replied, 'Well, I didn't have much on and I thought I'd come and see if you had any bargains.'

Uncle Theo threw back his head (not literally, you understand) and let out a laugh which shook the teacups back in the china department. 'Always. Always. You know that. Uncle Theo's always got bargains... and cap-it-al bargains too!' he beamed.

As Uncle Theo was speaking, we arrived at the 'Odds and Odder' collection. There was the usual pile of deviant bric-a-brac, but dominating the whole weird lot was a magnificent stuffed zebra. It had obviously not been fully grown when it met its end, but it stood nearly two metres tall and its face wore an expression which said, 'Please, take me home'.

I was hooked and, without any words having to be exchanged between us, Uncle Theo knew it!

'Well, me boy. What do you think of that? Came from an old gentleman's house in Cannington Crescent. His father had spent years in Africa and this was a kind of souvenir that he brought back.'

A sudden thought occurred to me. 'He didn't shoot it, did he?' I asked.

Uncle Theo was all calm reassurance. 'No bullet holes that I can see, Davey. Must have died of "natural causes", I suppose. But in one sense it lives on, doesn't it? Capital beast, I think. What about you?'

'Absolutely capital,' I muttered, still transfixed by the beast's magnetic attraction. I just *had* to have it, but my mind was racing ahead. How could I explain to Mum that I had spent my savings on a stuffed zebra? She wouldn't understand. She seems to think I should be saving up for going on holiday and stuff like that, but this was the chance of a lifetime. We go on holiday every single year, but I had never ever seen a stuffed zebra for sale before.

As I mused, some words came back to my mind. I usually close down the 'school' bit of my brain at weekends, but something about this zebra seemed to draw some school-related words back into my consciousness.

'Take... body... horse-like... mammal.'

Yes. 'Oh thank you, God,' I thought. Mum could never argue if it was for my homework. She was always saying that I didn't put enough effort into it. Well, this time I would do it properly. I would fulfil Mr Grimshaw's request to the letter. 'Body... horse-like... mammal' he wanted, and 'Body... horse-like... mammal' he would get!

'How much for the zebra, Uncle Theo?' I heard myself saying.

No, but seriously...

'Mum always warned me about going around with Dixy...'

Would you choose someone like Dixy to hang out with? There are good mates, OK mates and disastrous mates – and the choices you make about them can seriously affect your life.

If you want to think through choosing who your friends are, look at page 88.

If you want to think through choosing who your friends are, look at page 88.

* * * * * *

'I could almost feel this spending urge coming upon me...'

OK, own up. What do you spend your money on? CDs, clothes, sport, cinema, magazines... the list goes on and on. You need to know (if you don't already) that there is some big business out there targetting the pounds in your pockets. How are you going to decide when to spend it and what to spend it on?

For info on cash-related choices, turn to page 89.

On the other hand, if you're not really bothered, read on...

Chapter 4

As I walked home from Uncle Theo's Emporium, I just *knew* that I'd got a bargain. Uncle Theo had given me a generous 'family' discount and the zebra was mine for a mere £28.95. I'd already chosen a name for it. In fact, one look at it and there was only one name you *could* call it. Its curling mane standing up on top of its head and its turned-up top lip revealing a perfectly formed set of white teeth said 'Call me Elvis' as clearly as if the creature could speak. So, Elvis it was.

I couldn't wait to see Mum's face when I told her how seriously I was taking my Biology homework this time. No quick-fix ripping photos of 'horse-like mammals' out of the *TV Times* for me. Oh no. This was to be my finest hour. Mum would be delighted and I expected Mr Grimshaw would probably give me a Commendation!

'Hello, Mum. I'm home,' I yelled, as I walked in through the back door.

Mum was in the next room watching *Ready Steady Crook*, a programme about how to make a million pounds by fiddling your taxes, robbing banks and stuff like that. It was very popular, so popular with Mum in fact that she didn't hear me call.

I tried again. 'Hello. Earth to Mum. Are you receiving me?'

This time the signal got through. 'Is that you, David?

You've been gone a long time. Where have you been?' she enquired.

'I went to see Uncle Theo.'

The effect of mentioning Uncle Theo was dramatic. Mum shot up out of her chair, leaving the Ready Steady Crook presenter halfway through an explanation of how to print your own five-pound notes using nothing but a potato, beetroot juice and a steam iron.

'Oh you haven't, have you?' she asked, more in hope than expectation. 'What load of junk has he palmed off on you this time?'

I thought that there was an unfair implication in that question which did not deserve to go unchallenged, so I challenged it. 'No junk at all. Uncle Theo doesn't sell junk, he sells... first-rate quality goods at low, low prices,' I replied, deliberately using a favourite phrase of Uncle Theo's.

'Low, low quality goods at first-rate prices, more like,' muttered Mum. 'I don't believe you've come back with nothing. What is it this time?'

Mum's aggressive tone undermined my confidence that she'd understand about the zebra, but she would have to know sooner or later. I decided that 'sooner' was better than 'later', so I blurted out, 'A zebra.'

Mum's expression revealed that she clearly thought she hadn't heard right. She said, 'I beg your pardon? What did you say? For one minute I thought you said a zebra.' And she laughed at her own misunderstanding.

This was not going according to plan. I decided to give a full explanation, so that she could understand what a completely sensible and rational decision it had been to buy Elvis.

'Mum, I did say a zebra. Uncle Theo had this wonderful stuffed zebra – about this big.' I held my arms out to indicate Elvis' dimensions. Mum took a step back as I waved my arms, in the manner of one side-stepping a mad axeman running amok in a crowd, and I continued in a rush, 'Mr Grimshaw will be over the moon because Elvis came from Africa yonks ago and he's got the body of a horse-like mammal.'

My explanation clearly had not helped Mum to grasp the situation. Her forehead creased up in puzzled wonderment as she slowly worked her way over what I'd said.

'Mr Grimshaw's got the body of a horse-like mammal... Elvis Presley came from Africa...' She came closer to me and felt my forehead. 'Are you feeling all right, dear? You're not making a lot of sense, you know. Mind you, after spending a morning with my half-witted brother, I'm not surprised.'

I was exasperated at Mum's inability to grasp the basic facts of the matter. I tried again.

'Mum, I never mentioned *Elvis Presley*. Will you listen to me?' I spoke very slowly, pronouncing each syllable individually so as to make myself crystal clear.

'I have pur-chased a stuffed zeb-ra from Un-cle The-o. The zeb-ra is called El-vis. It came from A-fri-ca. It is for my Bi-ol-o-gy home-work. Mis-ter Grim-shaw told us to take in the bo-dy of a horse-like ma-mmal. Is... that... clear... e-nough... for... you?'

Mum didn't speak, she just looked. The look, however, did say a lot. Amongst other things it said,

'You are completely mad';
then it said,
'I'll kill that brother of mine';
then it said,
'I think I need to lie down.'

As Mum left the room, I was left to reflect on the sheer injustice of life. You cannot win. Elvis demonstrated the point perfectly. If you don't do your homework, you get grounded. If you rush your homework and do the bare minimum, you get an ear-bashing. If you buy a zebra and do your homework properly for once, you get the frosty reception and the icy stare. No justice at all.

In an attempt to pull the threads of my life back together again, I began to consider how to spend the rest of my day. I didn't have any plans but I didn't want to stay in the house and risk another emotionally charged encounter with Mum. I decided to give Kevin a ring; he always had plans.

'Three-two-seven-seven-nine-twohoo. Kevin-speaking-and-who-are-youhoo?'

'Hi! Kev, it's David. You doing anything? I'm so bored.'

Kevin, as I said, always had plans. 'Hey, you geek, don't say you've forgotten. You're such an airhead. Tonight's the night my parents are going out and I'm having a bit of a party. Gary and Rob Brand are coming and Gabby and Karen and some of their mates. I did tell you about it last week and you said you'd come.'

I had forgotten. With Kevin's parents out and the likes of Gary Mendham (who never went anywhere on a Saturday night without a six-pack of lager), it sounded like it could be a dodgy evening. But on the other hand, given recent developments, so could staying in with Mum and Dad (who had yet to hear about Elvis).

The thought of explaining to Dad that I had spent £28.95 on a stuffed zebra spurred me into making a snap decision.

'Oh yeah, right. Count me in. What time does it all happen?'

'Well, Mum and Dad have already gone out and they won't be back until gone midnight, so come round when you like.'

As I put the phone down I was already looking forward to the evening out, but not for the same reason that everyone else probably was. I ran over the list of probable party-goers in my mind, each with their own reason for descending on Kev's tonight.

Gabby Locke was probably looking forward to the party because she wanted to go out with Rob Brand and tonight gave her the chance to make her big move. Sadly for Gabby however, Rob Brand was probably looking forward to the party because he fancied Karen Box, who was probably looking forward to the party because she fancied Gary Mendham (at least as long as he kept her supplied with lager). Gary Mendham was looking forward to the party because he fancied lager, and himself.

It wasn't that I didn't fancy anyone at the moment. In fact, when I wasn't obsessed with zebras, Sophie Bromwell had become a bit of an obsession with me. She was very fanciable, but was unfortunately going out with Damon Dooley at the moment. However, I had been told that Damon Dooley now fancied Peter Vinshi's sister in Year 8, Vanessa. Now if Vanessa could only get her mind off Darren Baron and begin to appreciate the finer points of Damon Dooley, that would put Sophie Bromwell in need of a bit of tender loving care – a task for which I reckoned myself to be particularly well suited.

Anyway, the school fancying network is a bit complicated and as I say, apart from Sophie Bromwell, I had other things on my mind. I was looking forward to the party because this was to be my only chance to see my schoolmates before Monday morning, and I needed to recruit a zebra-removal gang to help me get Elvis from Uncle Theo's Emporium to school.

After a quick raid on the fridge for a bit of lunch, I made my way to Kev's. Kev opened the door with a 'Hi. Just in time', before scurrying back into his sitting room.

I followed him in and found that Rob had already arrived and was sat, remote control in hand, waiting to start the video he'd brought round.

He looked up as I entered. 'Hi, Dave,' he said, 'neat timing. Just about to press "play".'

'What's the film?' I asked. I knew that Rob's tastes weren't exactly the same as mine, so I thought it wise to check because it's amazing just how many 'tastes' there are in video-land.

There's 'the-aliens-have-landed-and-taken-over-Tescos' flavour which is my personal favourite. Then there's 'oh-no-can-he-find-the-bomb-before-it-blows-up-the-president's-trousers' flavour, much loved by Pete Miles. Always a favourite with Gabby's gang are the subtle flavours of 'I-love-her-but-she-loves-him-and-it'll-all-end-in-tears-because-he's-actually-the-brother-she-never-knew-she-had' while I knew that Kev's preference was for the decidedly more unsubtle 'gosh-this-is-funny-I-never-imagined-that-the-bucket-of-custard-would-land-on-the-man's-head'.

As for Rob's tastes, they could best be described as 'he's-been-beheaded-she's-been-stabbed-they've-had-their-legs-chewed-off-by-mutant-squirrels', so I waited to hear the video's title with the sort of feeling that you have when you ask why the health inspectors have just closed down your favourite pizza takeaway shop.

'It's called *Scream Through the Night and All the Next Day*, and it's about a family who live next door to these body-builders who are into Kung Fu, snake-handling and chainsaws. Should be good. You ready?' he asked, his finger poised over the 'Play' button.

Now it's not that I'm over-sensitive, and maybe it was because I still hadn't fully recovered from Mr Grimshaw's '18'-rated Biology lesson, but I have to confess that I was not ready to sit and watch two hours of *Scream Through the Night and All the Next Day*. I decided to play for time.

'Yeah. Sounds great.' (OK, I lied.) 'But shouldn't we wait for the others to get here? After all, it's a shame to waste such a great film on just three of us, especially as Kev's so thick he won't understand a word of it.'

It was said in fun as a deliberate attempt to wind up Kev, who rose to the bait magnificently.

'Who are you calling thick, swede-head?' he said, and threw a poorly-aimed cushion at my head.

It landed on Kev's mum's cat, Tigger, who clearly thought she was being mugged (or should that be mogged?) by a small, soft, square dog with no legs. She took off in terror, lapping the room at an amazing rate.

On the first lap, Tigger knocked over a vase of flowers and on her second, she cleared the ornaments from the mantelpiece. Kev and Rob took off after her to prevent any more damage, but it was an ill-fated plan because on Tigger's third and fastest circuit of the room, it was *them* who caused the damage, Kev putting his foot through the glass-topped coffee table and Rob ending up in the corner with the shade from the standard lamp stuck on his head.

The action ended as suddenly as it began. On her fourth lap, Tigger overdid the hairpin turn by the open door and span right through it before skidding to a halt upside down in a heap at the bottom of the stairs in the hallway. She quickly sat up, peered back through into the carnage of the sitting room before gliding upstairs to resume her nap.

Kev was furious and showed it. 'You stupid great idiot. Now look what you've done.'

I looked at Rob to see how he was receiving this accusation only to find him staring at me. The realisation that Kev held *me* responsible for the damage to his parents' front room was hard to take.

'What do you mean, what I've done? *You* threw the cushion. *You* hit the cat. *You* chased the cat. *You* put your foot through the coffee table.'

At the mention of the coffee table, Kev looked down at his leg and noticed for the first time that there was blood oozing through his trousers. For the second time in two days, Kevin Kavinsky passed out and hit the floor.

Rob and I managed to prop him up by the sofa and while Rob went to find a sticking plaster, I dabbed his forehead with my handkerchief dipped in the water from the spilt flower vase.

In no time at all, Rob returned with plasters from the bathroom cabinet and Kev had revived enough to inspect the damage. Despite the flow of blood which had suggested the laceration of a major artery, closer investigation revealed that it was only a small cut, and the application of a plaster soon covered the wound.

As we began to clear up, I silently reflected that despite the gruesome mess that had been created, at least I had been spared the even more gruesome messes of *Scream Through the Night and All the Next Day*. Kevin appeared to have lost all his appetite for bloodthirsty films; in fact, he had appeared to have lost all his appetite *full stop*.

It wasn't long before the room almost resembled the one that I had entered about an hour earlier. (Doesn't time fly when you're enjoying yourself?) Admittedly, some of the ornamental china horses on the mantelpiece had lost a limb or two, but the idea of disguising the hole in the coffee table where the glass panel had been with a tea towel pressed into service as an emergency tablecloth was brilliant. (Or at least it was, until Kev came into the room and placed the vase that he had been, painstakingly glueing back together in the kitchen on the coffee table, only to see it disappear straight through the concealed hole and smash for a second time on the floor!)

Order had been restored in absolute silence, but now that we had nearly finished, I decided to spring my exciting news on Kev and Rob in an attempt to cheer them up.

'Hey, you'll never guess what,' I began.

'So why ask?' responded Kevin, still sulkily rubbing his damaged ankle.

I continued, despite this grouchy response. 'No, listen. I spent the morning at my Uncle Theo's shop. You know, the mad one who owns that second-hand shop down Parson's Street.'

Rob chipped in. 'I know the place you mean. I didn't know your uncle owned it. What does he look like? I got ripped off there once by some big geezer wearing a kilt. He sold me a video called *Blood up to Your Elbows* which he said was the most scary thing he'd ever seen. "Capitally creepy", I think he called it. But when I got it home it was just a training film for people who work in butchers' shops. Right royal rip-off.'

I chose not to identify Uncle Theo as the video salesman in question but hastened on.

'Yeah, well, like I said, my Uncle Theo owns the shop and he has all sorts of weird stuff there, and you'll never guess what I bought this morning – so I'll tell you.' I paused to heighten the effect of the announcement, then proceeded. 'A zebra.'

Kev spoke first, his grumpiness temporarily suspended by his interest in what I'd said.

'I beg your pardon. What did you say? For one minute I thought you said a zebra.' And he laughed at his own misunderstanding.

I had been here before. I'd expected better of my own mates but I needed their help so I persevered. 'I *did* say a zebra, you gibbering idiot. A real-life stuffed zebra, called Elvis.'

Neither of them noticed the contradiction in terms; they were too agog at the thought that their mate, who they thought they knew, had gone and bought a zebra.

'What on earth for? I mean, like... why?' Rob's voice trailed off into wondering disbelief.

'Well, because I liked it. Why do you buy all those grotty videos? And more to the point, because I'm going to take it in to Mr Grimshaw for our Biology homework. And what is more, you are both going to help me do it.'

No, but seriously....

'The school fancying network is a bit complicated...'

Who do you fancy? Anyone? No one? Everyone?! Sometimes you can get the feeling that if you're not going out with someone (or at least working at it), there must be something very wrong with you. Is that true?

For help on choosing who to ask out (or not), see page 90.

* * * * * *

'It's amazing just how many tastes there are in video-land...'

What about your viewing preferences? Do you prefer thrillers, romances, horror or comedy? What do you choose to watch — and do you always feel good about your choice by the end of the film?

For ideas about choosing your viewing, see page 91.

On the other hand, if you're not really bothered, read on...

Chapter 5

Ohhhh! *D-a-a-d*!! Today's wake-up shower-song went to the tune of 'Happy Birthday':

> *'Sunday morning again,*
> *And I can't explain*
> *Why I'm in my shower*
> *And not out in Spain.'*
> (Repeat 20 million times.)

My sleep-befuddled mind slowly began to locate itself in the universe. Place? My bed. Time? A quick peer at my clock revealed that it was 8.00 am. Day? Sunday.

What happened yesterday? Wide-awakeness arrived in a moment as I remembered Saturday's sequence of events: the trip to Uncle Theo's, my first meeting with Elvis, Mum's less-than-enthusiastic response followed by the chaos caused by Kev's cat. It had been some day!

It had probably been some evening at Kev's too, but after the 'cat incident', I somehow didn't feel very welcome there and having got a grudging commitment from Kev and Rob to help me shift Elvis on Monday morning, I left before the others arrived and came home early to mug up on zebras on my dad's computer.

A bit of rambling around the Worldwide Web and I found an ace site that had just about everything about zebras that anyone could ever want to know. For instance, did you know that a tip-top zebra can travel at 40 miles per hour, that no two zebras have the same pattern of stripes and that they're such friendly beasts that they sometimes hang around in groups with up to 1,000 of their mates?

Anyway, that was yesterday, but as I gradually came to this morning, a strange dream that I'd had last night came back to me.

My class were all sitting in Miss Pugh's classroom, but it wasn't Miss Pugh at the front, it was my dad. He was standing in a shower cubicle at the front of the room singing Elvis Presley songs to us. It was really embarrassing, but as I looked round I realised that no one could hear him, because instead of ears everyone had two enormous eyes on the sides of their heads. I was sitting next to Gary Mendham, who for some reason was covered in sticking plasters, and he passed me some extra-strength lager in a distinctive black and white can. As I tugged the ring-pull, Mr Grimshaw came out of the can. At least it was Mr Grimshaw's head but the body was that of a strange horse-like mammal which was wearing a kilt. As I watched, the tartan-clad Mr Grimshaw-type beast approached my dad, bit his head off and swallowed it whole. This last bit happened several times because my dad's head kept growing back, each time with a louder voice.

They say that all dreams mean something. I'm not sure what that one means but I *hope* it means that if my dad doesn't stop singing in the shower, something ghastly is going to happen to him!

Now fully awake, I was ready for my breakfast. On most days breakfast is a bit of a haphazard, grab-a-bowl-of-Shreddies-as-you-rush-for-the-bus affair. On Sundays, however, we all sit down together to eat; it's one of those family-bonding things that Dad read about once in one of his *Reader's Digest* magazines.

'We all' includes Mum, Dad and me, who you've met, plus my little brother, who I've deliberately kept quiet about.

Tom is a ten-year-old pain and I feel much the same way about him that Mum feels about Uncle Theo. Inter-brother relations were not improved this morning by my discovery that Tom, who had beaten me to the breakfast table, had opened the new box of Bite-Size Krrrunchy Choco-Hoops and was brandishing the plastic model of Captain Zoggwart from that new TV space series.

(You may remember that Captain Zoggwart was the one who threw himself into the synthetic protolapse time chasm in an heroic attempt to save the Mekonites from the laser-guided death rays of the invading Gringlewok intergalactic raiding party whose advance guard of alien warriors had already taken over Tesco's. On the other hand, you may not.)

Anyway, at the moment Captain Zoggwart was the only missing piece of my 'Marvellous Mekonite Models' collection. In an attempt to get him, I had eaten my way through seven boxes of Bite-Size Krrrunchy Choco-Hoops in the last two weeks, sometimes resorting to sneaking downstairs in the middle of the night to finish a box just so that I could legitimately open the new box and rummage through its contents.

And now Tom, who knew how much Captain Zoggwart meant to me, was sitting there waving him round his head and yelling, 'I've got Captain Zoggwart. I've got Captain Zoggwart.'

I just had to respond, so I said, 'That's not fair! You

know I need him. You're not even collecting them. Give him here.'

I might as well have said 'Fly round the room', because there was no way Tom was going to give up his prize find.

'No way! I found him and I'm keeping him,' was Tom's taunting response.

I am not a violent person but reasoning with Tom was not going to get me anywhere and since Mum and Dad were both temporarily out of the room, I decided to solve this problem in the quickest way possible. I set my spoon to 'stun' and hit Tom on the back of the hand that was holding Captain Zoggwart captive. The blow made Tom involuntarily open his hand and Captain Zoggwart was free-falling to the floor without even a parachute to slow him down (a typically heroic manoeuvre).

Tom and I both dived to retrieve the model at the same time and there was a sickening thud as our heads crashed together. I fell back onto my chair, stunned, but Tom fell onto the floor, taking the tablecloth, assorted bowls, spoons, cereal boxes and marmalade pots with him.

It made quite a noise, but it was nothing compared to the noise that Dad made when he rushed into the room to discover the cause of the commotion.

Fortunately for Tom, the tablecloth had completely covered him, hiding him on the floor. I, on the other hand, was sitting directly in Dad's line of sight, rubbing the emerging lump on my head.

'*Da-vid*!! What *are* you doing? Whatever has been going on here? Look at this mess and where's Tom gone?'

A ghastly moaning sound wafted out from underneath the debris on the floor and Tom's head appeared from under the cloth.

Mum came in.

'Oh Tom, are you all right? What's happened?' She helped Tom to his feet and immediately began applying margarine to the lump on his forehead. (Don't ask me what good it's supposed to do, but my family has always put margarine on bumped heads.)

She turned to me or, to be more accurate, she turned *on* me.

'How could you? How *could* you be so stupid? Look what you've done to his head. This lump is swelling up like a melon. I don't know what's got into you lately but you'd better start pulling yourself together, my boy.' (Whenever Mum called me her 'boy', I knew I was in *big* trouble.) She was in full flow and her anger was still rising. 'All you had to do was to sit at the breakfast table and wait for a few short minutes while Dad and I got ready. But can you do it? No, oh no. Not you. *When* are you going to grow up?'

It wasn't really a question, more an accusation – an expression of her shock at finding the breakfast on the floor and Tom's head swelling up like a balloon, I suppose. It would have been better to stay quiet, but Mum and Dad's immediate assumption that I had been responsible for the incident upset my sense of justice so I protested:

'For goodness' sake, it wasn't *my* fault! Why do I get blamed for everything round here? How come Tom gets away with everything and I get blamed for everything? It's always the same.'

Dad weighed in. 'That's not true, David.'

'Yes it is,' I snapped back. Bad move.

Dad's voice remained calm but there was that look on his face which said, 'I'm saying something here that you ignore or argue with at your peril. Listen to what I'm saying or wash up for a week.' I listened.

'No it's not, David. You're angry and probably feeling guilty about what you've done, so I want you to go to your room and cool down for ten minutes while Mum and I clear up the mess you've made. When we've finished, I'll call you back down and we'll start breakfast again.'

Ten minutes cooling down wasn't enough. I had gone over the incident a million times in that ten minutes and each time I became even more convinced that I had done nothing wrong. So it was that I was still fuming at the injustice of the situation when I was called back to the breakfast table. We all ate in tense silence, no one daring to speak in case they said something to reignite the smouldering fires of anger that for different reasons we all felt. So much for family-bonding breakfasts!

To compound the misery, this was Sunday and for the next two hours we would all be thrown together being artificially nice to each other at church.

Our church was one of those new sorts that don't have a building, don't have a vicar, don't use hymn books and don't finish until gone 12.30. We meet in a school hall which is transformed into a place of worship every Sunday morning by a gang of willing volunteers who put out chairs for the congregation, PA equipment for the worship band and notice-sheets for the Sunday School kids to make into paper aeroplanes.

As Dad pulled into the car park of Greenbank School, I was out of the car almost before the wheels had stopped turning. It wasn't that I was especially keen to get into church this morning, but I went on ahead to avoid arriving in the hall with Mum, Dad and Tom, whose forehead now looked like it was about to give birth to a tennis ball.

In the foyer I was welcomed by Bill, our youth leader.

He was probably in his forties, looked like he was in his thirties, dressed like he was in his twenties and acted like he was a teenager. He always wore a baseball cap, pushed back on his shaved head. From his ear dangled an earring which brushed the upturned collar of his leather jacket when he turned his head.

'Yo, smack-it! 'Ow's ya rollin'?' he asked in Youth Leader-speak. (He wanted to know how I was but for some reason thought that if he said, 'Hello, Dave. How are you this morning?' I wouldn't be able to understand him.)

'I'm OK,' I lied. I was trying to forget all about the fact that I had a family, so I wasn't about to explain the Big Breakfast Bust-Up to Bill. Instead, I tried to introduce the new love of my life into the conversation. 'Had a good day yesterday. Went shopping.'

Bill was interested. 'That's razor sharp, Dave. Crack any eggs? Crop any circles? Know what I mean?'

I had no idea what he meant but I took it as an invitation to tell him what I'd bought, so I continued, 'I bought a zebra from my Uncle Theo's shop.'

Bill was so taken aback that he spoke in English. 'I beg your pardon. What did you say? For one minute I thought you said a zebra.' And he laughed at his own misunderstanding.

This was getting tiresome. First Mum, then Kev and Rob and now Bill. What was wrong with everyone?

'I *did* say a zebra. We needed one for our homework and, guess what, I found one – probably the only one in the whole town – in my Uncle Theo's shop. I hadn't prayed about it or anything but God must have known what I needed before I got round to mentioning it to him.' I tried to slip something spiritual into the conversation to show Bill that I prayed between youth group meetings. (Actually, the last time I prayed about anything was when I prayed that Tom would turn into a woodlouse, so that I could stand on him and pretend I'd only meant to trip him up. It hadn't worked.)

Disappointingly, Bill seemed slightly less convinced about God's participation in my shopping expedition. He said, 'It's poss. Weird stuff for homework, or what!' A further thought occurred to him. 'Is Zeb up to the walk to school or do you need wheels?'

He obviously hadn't grasped that Uncle Theo's shop was a junk, er... second-hand goods shop and not a pet shop. I straightened him out.

'Bill, get a grip. The zebra's dead...'

'Hey, heavy duty distress, man. Like, I'm sorry,' he said awkwardly.

Bill's interruption got me a bit flustered so I said, 'No, not *dead*-dead...Well, yes, it is dead, but it was never alive.'

'Spoooo-ky. A Zeb from Zorg. That's some beast you got yourself.'

It was like talking to your worst nightmare! I tried just one more time to get the story straight in such a way that even Bill could grasp the basics.

'Bill, pay attention. Watch my lips if it helps. The zebra which, a long time ago, was alive, is now dead. But it wasn't buried and forgotten about. It was preserved and stuffed. It ended up in my uncle's second-hand shop and I bought it. Tomorrow morning I'm going to take it to school to show to Mr Grimshaw. Got it?'

As I explained, light had dawned on Bill's face so I carried on and answered his question of a few moments earlier.

'As to whether or not I need "wheels", I'm not sure. I've been thinking about how to get it to school. I've got two of my mates turning up to help me, but beyond that I'm a bit stuck. Got any ideas?'

Now I knew that Bill had a large van which he used to take camping stuff on our youth weekends away (amongst other things) and I was kind of hoping that he might offer to help. He didn't disappoint.

'I'm your man with a van, Dave. Name your time and place and consider it done.'

The service was about to start, so I hastily scribbled a map to Uncle Theo's shop on the back of a church notice-sheet and went into the hall which was by now quite full.

The service began as the worship band introduced the first song, following which Mr Johnstone, one of the people that helped in the Sunday School, went to the front.

'Now, it's nice to see so many children here this morning and we'd like you to help us with our prayers today,' he beamed encouragingly. 'We're going to say "thank you prayers" and "please prayers", and we'd like you to tell us what you want to thank God for and what you would like to ask him for.'

It was a nice idea. It got people involved and several young hands shot up. Peter Farmer wanted to thank God for the nice sunny day but Jessica Vingay wanted to ask God to make it rain so that she didn't have to go on a picnic with her parents that afternoon.

'It will be interesting to see how God sorts that one out,' I thought.

However, their apparently contradictory prayers were written up alongside the several other suggestions that had already been displayed for all to see on the overhead projector.

Things were quietening down as we sensed the prayers about to begin and, with hindsight, it would have been better if Mr Johnstone had left it there. But in an attempt to include some of the older teenagers in the process, he made one last request.

'Now what about some of you older ones? Haven't you got anything to thank God for or to ask him?' Apparently not, since silence reigned. He decided to press the point.

'What about you, David? Has anything happened that you'd like to thank God for or to ask him to do?'

I don't know what made me say it. But to my horror I heard myself announcing the honest prayers of my heart in front of the whole church. 'Yeah, actually there is. Thanks for my zebra and please would my little brother drop dead.'

No, but seriously...

'Tom is a 10 year old pain...'

OK, so you've got the perfect relationship with your little brother or sister. You never argue, never fight, never get jealous of one another and always feel that your parents treat you both fairly.

In that case you can ignore page 92. If, on the other hand, you sometimes wish you had made different choices in your relationship with little bro or sis, turn to page 92 now.

* * * * * *

'It's not that I really wanted to go to church...'

Do you go to church? Do you *choose* to go to church? Do you choose *which* church to go to? Are you happy that the church you go to is the best choice for you?

Sometimes people choose to give up on church altogether when all they needed to do was choose a church that suited them better – or maybe just choose to try a bit harder in the church that they were already in. To think through churchy-choices, turn to page 93.

If, on the other hand, you're not really bothered, read on...

Chapter 6

'You said *what*?! What happened then?'

For the first time ever, Kev was interested in what happened at our church. Mum and Dad had gone out for a walk by the canal with Tom (hope he falls in) and I had phoned Kev to help pass the long Sunday afternoon. Being grounded on a Sunday can seem like for ever!

'Well, there was kind of a pause during which I suppose everyone was kind of processing what I'd said. Then all the youth group burst out laughing and cheering and yelling, "Nice one, Dave" and stuff like that...'

Kev cut in, sounding a bit disappointed. 'So everyone was pleased with what you'd said?'

I thought about the embarrassed looks on the faces of the adults near me, the helpless look on Mr Johnstone's face and the murderous look on Mum's.

'Well, not exactly *everyone*...' I paused before setting the record straight. 'In fact, hardly anyone at all really.'

Kev was more upbeat. 'It sounds cool to me. After all, that's what you wanted to pray about, wasn't it? If you believe God knows everything anyway, what's the point of pretending when you speak to him?'

For someone who claimed that he didn't know what he believed about 'God and stuff' (as he put it), Kev could come up with some pretty astute observations! .

I decided to move the conversation away from church to the subject which had begun to take over my whole attention: that of moving Elvis from Uncle Theo's shop to school by 8.45 tomorrow morning.

'You still OK for tomorrow morning?' I asked. 'We'll need to make an early start. Can you be at Uncle Theo's by half past seven?' 'In the morning' I added, just to make sure that Kev had grasped the full implications of what I was asking.

'*Half past seven in the morning*?' Kev sounded as though I'd just asked him to chop his legs off with a blunt penknife. 'You must be joking. And anyway, I didn't *definitely* say I'd help shift your zebra. I only said I might.'

Now that was not on, since I distinctly remember Kev agreeing to help.

'Oh, come on, Kev,' I urged. 'Don't let me down now. It's all set up. Rob's coming and Bill's turning up with his van.'

Kevin thawed a bit when he heard that transport arrangements had been made, but it was still with some reluctance in his voice that he conceded, 'OK then. But there aren't many people who I'd get up at that time of day for.'

Good old Kev! I knew I could rely on him. A further thought crossed my mind and, having got Kev's agreement to be involved this far, I thought I'd risk another request.

'Could you call round for Rob on your way? You know what he's like at getting up in the morning, and if you call for him it'll be a bit of insurance that he actually gets there.'

Kev agreed and I put the phone down, reflecting on how good it was to have mates who would stand by you in a time of need. The rest of the day passed impossibly slowly. Not only was I grounded for my honesty in church, but I was banned from watching TV as well. With nothing else to do and with the prospect of an early start tomorrow, I took myself off to bed at 9 o'clock.

★ ★ ★ ★ ★ ★ ★ ★ ★ ★ ★ ★ ★ ★ ★ ★

'Splash it here, splash it there,
Splash it nearly everywhere.
Aftershave is smelly,
Slap some on my belly,
Now I'm ready to go off to work.'
(To the tune of 'Postman Pat'. Repeat 34 million times.)

Today I didn't object to the early morning call. Today was going to be ace and even Dad's singing couldn't spoil it. I was looking forward to it all, from the journey to school in Bill's van to the look on Mr Grimshaw's face when I showed him my homework in this morning's science lesson. What would he say, I wondered? Probably something like, 'That is most impressive, David. I really didn't expect anyone to come up with a *real* body of a horse-like mammal. You have obviously put a lot of effort into your homework this time. I should think that this should put you in line for a Gold Commendation at least.'

Anyway, all that was for later. Right now was the time to get up and try to sneak out of the house without arousing too much parental suspicion. To be strictly honest, I hadn't fronted up to my early morning activities with Mum and Dad. After the shocked response from Mum when I'd first told her about Elvis, I'd hardly mentioned the subject for fear of causing more grief to fall on my head. I was sort of hoping that she might have forgotten all about my plan to take Elvis to school.

As I crept downstairs, fully dressed for school at 6.45 am, I was pretty certain that Mum would still be in bed, which meant that I would only have to bluff my way around Dad, who by now had finished showering and was in the kitchen.

'Hi, Dad,' I said, sounding as cheerily natural as I could for one who usually couldn't be scraped out of bed by 7.30. Dad had been slurping his wake-up cup of coffee with his back to me as I'd entered the kitchen, and my chirpy greeting had the effect of startling him into spilling some of the hot liquid onto his slippered feet.

'Owwww! Owwwww!' he yelled, as he hopped wildly all across the kitchen, bent double, snatching his slippers and then his socks from his feet and flinging them across the room. Somehow, despite his obvious discomfort, he hopped to the sink, filled the washing-up bowl with cold water, placed it on the floor, rolled up his trouser legs and stood in the bowl to alleviate the pain of the scalding coffee. From this less-than-dignified position, for the first time, he spoke to me. The tone was not friendly.

'What on earth are you doing up at this time of day? And what do you mean by sneaking up on me like that? Of all the silly, stupid, childish things to do, that... that... that just about takes the gold medal!'

Fortunately, as his feet began to cool down, so did his anger and he kind of ground to a halt at that stage. His curiosity, however, was still red-hot and so he repeated his first question.

'Well, just what are you doing up at this time of day?'

He glared at me, feet still firmly planted in the washing-up bowl.

'I'm just off to school, Dad. I've got to go in a bit early today,' I said, trying to bend the truth as little as possible.

'A *little* early. This is almost a whole *hour* before you even get out of bed on a usual school day. So what's the big idea?' he persisted.

'Well, it's to do with some homework that I've got to do for Mr Grimshaw,' I continued, still hovering near the truth. Unfortunately, Dad's less-than-satisfied expression demanded more of an explanation and I found myself plunging into downright deceit. 'Mr Grimshaw asked us to get into school early so that he could collect in our homework before he goes off on a science trip with the sixth form.'

Dad seemed to accept the right of teachers to impose any conditions they liked on the collecting of homework.

'Oh well, if Mr Grimshaw says so, I suppose you'd better go,' he said, now standing on one foot in the bowl while gingerly patting the other one dry with a tea towel.

As I raced down the road, I glanced at my watch. The hoo-ha with Dad had slowed me up a bit. It was twenty past seven but I should still just make it before Bill, Kev and Rob arrived. As I entered Parson's Street and saw the shabby shopfront of Uncle Theo's Emporium, I suddenly became aware of a gigantic flaw in my planning for this morning's enterprise. I had arranged to get myself up early. I had arranged for Kev and Rob to turn up and help. I had arranged transport in Bill's van, but I had completely forgotten to take account of the fact that at 7.30 am Uncle Theo's shop was shut! What a wally!

Fortunately, as I've told you, Uncle Theo lives in the flat above his shop so he wasn't far away, but it would mean getting him up and that would waste valuable time. However, a quick consideration of the other options revealed that there *were* no other options, so I ran down the alleyway beside the shop, raced up the steps to Uncle Theo's flat and pressed the doorbell.

I could hear the dull chimes of 'Amazing Grace' through Uncle Theo's half-glazed door as his electronic 'Chime-a-Toon' doorbell attempted to rouse him from his slumber. I peered through the frosted glass. No sign of movement, so I pressed the bell again and started verse two of the well-known hymn. Still no movement.

It was well into verse six before Uncle Theo's towering silhouette appeared at the other side of the door. A rattling of security chains preceded the door being prised open just enough for Uncle Theo's face to peer out.

Despite the hour and the fact that I'd just woken him up, he still managed to boom welcomingly, 'Davey, me boy! What are you doing here at this time of day?'

The door was thrown fully open to reveal Uncle Theo resplendent in his tartan dressing gown. He scratched his head and said, 'Actually, come to mention it, what time of day *is* it?'

I glanced at my watch again. It was twenty to eight! It had taken ten minutes to rouse Uncle Theo. Rob, Kev and Bill would be waiting round at the front by now. Things had to start moving a bit quicker or else we wouldn't get Elvis to school before registration.

I launched straight into my explanation. 'Uncle Theo, I'm really sorry to wake you up but I need to get Elvis — I mean, my zebra — out of your shop and take him to school with me. I've got some mates waiting to help round the front, so if you could just unlock the shop for a minute, I'd be really grateful.'

Uncle Theo looked delighted to be in on my exciting enterprise (or maybe he was just pleased to get rid of the zebra from his shop). Whatever the reason, he sprang into action. Grabbing his shop keys from the hook where they hung in his hallway, he strode along the corridor and down the stairs leading to Parson's Street and his shopfront. I followed behind.

As we entered the street I was somewhat perplexed to see that, apart from two cats and a milk float, there was no one else in sight. Where were Kev and Rob? Typical of them to be late! But what about Bill? I'd expected that *he* would be on time.

Uncle Theo unlocked his shop and I followed him back to where Elvis was standing with a 'SOLD' sticker on his nose. It may have been my imagination but it seemed like he winced as I yanked the label off, so I offered an apology.

'Sorry, Elvis. Remember me? I'm your new master – but you can call me Dave. I hope you've had your breakfast because this is your first day at school and I'm not sure you'll like school dinners very much.'

I patted his stomach area just to make sure he was well fed before his first journey in many a month. He seemed to be quite full ('stuffed' might be the word in fact), so I reckoned that he was just about ready to go. But where *were* the others? I'd just have to start moving Elvis out of the shop myself and hopefully they'd arrive in time to help me put him in the van.

Uncle Theo agreed to help and so we carefully manoeuvred Elvis down the narrow gangways of the shop and out onto the pavement. He looked a fine sight in the morning sunlight (Elvis, that is, not Uncle Theo), but as I checked the time and saw that it was now five to eight and there was still no sign of my so-called friends, I began to get a little anxious.

'Perhaps they've overslept, Davey,' suggested Uncle Theo, who'd noticed me anxiously glancing from my watch to the end of the road and back to my watch again. 'What are you going to do? Have you got a Plan B if they don't show up?' he asked.

No, I hadn't got a Plan B. But one was forming in my mind. It had nothing to do with removing Elvis but everything to do with revenge against Kev and Rob and Bill. How *could* they let me down like this? They'd promised to help (well, virtually promised), and now they weren't anywhere to be seen. My mind had begun to work out lavish and savage ways of getting even, involving poisoned packed lunches and punctured van tyres, when (mercifully) Uncle Theo interrupted again.

'Well, Davey, what *are* you going to do? I can't stand around here in my dressing gown all morning.'

He had a point but there was no way I could move Elvis on my own, so I said, 'I don't know, Uncle Theo. Elvis is too heavy for me to move on my own. If only he was on wheels I might manage it, but...'

'Capital idea, Davey. Cap-it-al!' Uncle Theo dived back into his shop, calling over his shoulder, 'I've got it. Wait right there...'

Seconds later he emerged, still talking, with a pair of skis, four ancient skateboards and a ball of string.

'Just what you need. We can tie the zebra to the skis with this string and then tie the skis to the skateboards. I reckon that'll mean that you can rock and roll your Elvis all the way to school with no trouble at all – all by yourself!'

I wasn't convinced at first, but with Uncle Theo's help we managed to secure Elvis to his own set of customised wheels and, after a few practice shoves up and down the pavement, I reckoned that it actually might work. Under normal circumstances it was about twenty minutes' walk to school from Uncle Theo's, but with Elvis in tow that would add about another ten minutes. It was by now 8.15 so I should just make it. Without wasting any more time, I set off.

By the time I'd got to the end of Parson's Street I'd already worked out that it was better to push Elvis than to pull him. For one thing, when you pulled him, his rear end had the habit of shooting sideways across the pavement, knocking into anything or anyone who happened to be standing too close.

And for another thing, by pushing, I could hide behind him and remain almost invisible (or so I hoped) as we made our way down the busy pavements towards school, leaving Elvis to confront the unbelieving stares of passers-by (he was really cool – he didn't blink once!).

Sadly, however, every silver lining has a cloud, and the disadvantage to pushing over pulling was that from behind Elvis' hindquarters, I had a very limited field of forward vision. That in turn meant that not infrequently Elvis would barge into some poor unsuspecting pedestrian who would turn to complain, only to find a zebra staring right back at them. Some screamed, some just gasped, but it was when one elderly lady fainted and nearly fell into the path of an oncoming bus that I realised that, after all, this was not going to work.

I peered out from behind Elvis and noticed that there was a phone box a little further along the pavement. I left Elvis watching the small crowd that were watching him, and with as much dignity as I could muster, made my way to the phone box.

Fortunately I knew Bill's phone number by heart. Maybe, just maybe, he was still at home and could even now, come to my rescue. I punched in 889913 and waited as the phone rang in Bill's house.

After a few rings a familiar voice said, 'Hiya. This is Billy. Rap on my friend.'

All my anger, frustration and anxiety came to the surface. '*Bill!*' I almost shouted. 'What are you doing *there?*'

After a slight pause, Bill, having given himself time to think about it, said, 'Hey, like... I'm answering the phone. Is that a problem?'

I tried again. 'Bill, *why* are you there answering the phone?'

Another pause.

'Well... hey, man... like... it rang, you know?'

Clearly I needed to postpone the tough questions until later – it was time for clarity.

'Bill, this is David, from church. You were supposed to help me move my zebra this morning. Remember?'

I could hear Bill muttering, 'Hey... like... you were *serious*?' but I cut across him.

'Listen, there's no time for apologies...' (not that one was being offered). 'I'm in a fix. Is it too late for you to get your van down to the phone box in Middleton Street to pick up me and my zebra?'

It was with great relief that I heard Bill say, 'Hang loose and peel a prawn, Davey. Startin' to groove, startin' to move.'

As I put the receiver back on its hook, I hoped that meant that Bill was on his way.

No, but seriously...

'I found myself plunging into downright deceit...'

Do you think it's a good thing to tell lies?   YES/NO

Do you like it when people lie to you or
tell lies about you?   YES/NO

Do you ever tell lies?   YES/NO

Let me guess. You answered 'No', 'No' and 'Yes'.
Crazy or what? Everyone thinks telling lies is a bad
thing to do and everyone hates it when other people
tell lies to or about them – but we all do it!

So why do we choose to tell untruths, and is it
always wrong to tell a lie anyway? For the truth about
lies, turn to page 94.

For the truth about lies, turn to page 94.

* * * * * *

'My mind had begun to work out lavish and savage
ways of getting even...'

'Don't get cross – get even!' Is that good advice? It
can certainly seem welcome advice when someone
lets us down badly or does something to hurt us. Our
natural response is to choose to get revenge, but is
that the only choice we could make? For ideas about
a better way of responding to life's disappointing
knocks, turn to page 95.

turn to page 95.

If, on the other hand, this isn't scratching where you
itch at the moment, read on...

Chapter 7

By the time Bill's white van screeched to a halt it was 8.40, and with registration due to start in just five minutes, I knew that I was going to be late for school. Fortunately Elvis had drawn quite a crowd, several of whom were keen to help Bill and me load him into the van, so it was not long before we were speeding off towards school.

As we pulled into the car park, it occurred to me that I would need somewhere to leave Elvis until Science, which was timetabled for second lesson. For the first time that day something went my way, because there on the playing field next to the car park stood Mr Timms, our sports teacher. Mr Timms was generally considered to be a 'top bloke' and so I had no hesitation in approaching him for a favour.

'Sir, hey, Mr Timms,' I called. 'Couldn't do us a favour could you, sir?'

Mr Timms looked up and walked towards me. 'That depends on what sort of favour you would like,' he replied.

'Well, Mr Grimshaw wanted me to bring in this rather unusual thing and I need somewhere to keep it until second lesson. I sort of wondered whether I could use the PE store,' I explained.

'For Mr Grimshaw? I don't see why not,' he said. And then he asked, 'What sort of unusual thing would it be?'

I took a deep breath and said, 'A zebra.'

I waited for Mr Timms to say, 'I beg your pardon? What did you say? I thought you said a zebra', and to laugh at his own misunderstanding – but he didn't. He just said, 'Cool. You know where I keep the key to the store, don't you?', and walked back to check the depth of the sand in the long jump pit (or whatever PE teachers do when they're not actually teaching).

Everyone else was in registration by now so the school grounds were actually quite quiet. Without more ado, Bill and I wheeled Elvis to the PE store and stowed him away, whereupon Bill drove off and I headed to the school office to sign in the Late Book, which we have to fill in if we miss registration.

Having done my duty at the office, I headed to join my class for first lesson – PSE. PSE actually stands for Personal and Social Education and according to the school prospectus it is supposed to help us 'discover ourselves and our place in the world'. We all reckon it really stands for Pretty Stupid Exercises because all we ever do is, well, one pretty stupid exercise after another.

Despite being a little late, I actually still arrived before Mrs Cooke, our PSE teacher, and so was spared the need to explain myself. A quick glance around the room revealed that both Kev and Rob were present, chatting away as though they hadn't just been the cause of the most stressful hour and a half of my life. All my feelings of anger, betrayal and revenge began to rise up but just as I was about to rush across the room and confront the guilty pair, Mrs Cooke arrived and I had to slip into a chair at the back and simmer quietly.

As the lesson started, my anger began to dissolve and I actually began to feel quite cheery. Well, why not? Despite the fact that everything had gone wrong this morning, I was still in school in time to start first lesson and, just as importantly, Elvis was in school ready to start second lesson. Maybe life wasn't so bad after all.

It was hard to concentrate on today's Pretty Stupid Exercises, but nevertheless I had to appear to be joining in. The point of it all (according to Mrs Cooke) was to help us begin to discover the sorts of career best suited to our individual abilities and personalities.

To make this vital discovery, we had to answer a sheet of about 100 questions such as, 'Do you prefer (a) to be indoors, or (b) outdoors?'; 'Do you like to work (a) alone, or (b) with others?' and 'Do you prefer (a) making things or (b) destroying things?'.

The only honest answer to all of the questions was '(c) It all depends'. For example, whether or not I prefer to be indoors or outdoors all depends on whether the indoors is at school or at home. At home I'd sooner be indoors watching TV than outdoors washing Dad's car, but at school I'd rather be outdoors playing football than indoors doing Pretty Stupid Exercises.

As to working alone or with others, it all depends on who the others are. If the others are real brainboxes and they help me get everything right without having to do much by myself, then of course I prefer to work with others. But if, on the other hand, they are all about as bright as a torch with no batteries, then I'd sooner take my risks on my own.

And with reference to making things or destroying things, once again, it all depends. If I'm given the choice of making a million quid or destroying a Cadbury's Creme Egg, then obviously I'd go for 'making things'. But if the choice is between making my bed and destroying Kev and Rob, then obviously (at the moment) I would choose 'destroying things'.

You see, it all depends.

However, '(c) It all depends' wasn't an option in this morning's Pretty Stupid Exercise, so we all duly chose either (a) or (b) and then Mrs Cooke helped us mark our answers to give us a points score at the end.

She then handed out another piece of paper which had a list of the sorts of jobs that might suit us, according to the number of points that we scored in the PSE. It was pretty clever stuff and opened our eyes to previously unconsidered career possibilities for which we were (apparently) almost perfectly suited.

For example, Sophie Brophy had never really considered a job in a coal mine, nor had Darren Baron (who was so afraid of heights that he got dizzy on a thick carpet) seriously considered being an airline pilot, but it seemed like they were each perfectly suited to those occupations.

Vegetarian though she was, Lucy Huntly would (it appears) feel quite at home working in an abattoir and I was delighted to discover that I was perfectly suited to being either a ballet dancer or someone who painted white lines down the middle of roads (both apparently required good balance, physical strength and the ability to ignore what other people thought about you). So it was that the lesson ended with our minds stirred to consider challenges that we had previously thought were beyond us.

However, ballet dancing and white-line painting aside, my main challenge now was to rescue Elvis from the sports store, and to do that I needed help. Despite my feelings of anger, I had worked out that my best bet was still Kev, who at least knew all about Elvis and wouldn't need to be convinced that he actually existed. I waited outside Mrs Cooke's room as my class filed out and when Kev appeared through the doorway, I pounced.

'Quite some mate you are, Kevin Cop-Out Kavinsky! Where were you this morning?' I stormed.

Kev looked a bit sheepish. 'I'm really sorry, Dave, but I overslept and then my mum wanted an explanation for why half her ornaments had lumps missing off them. Apparently she only noticed them last night and then... Well, you know how things are... Sorry,' he finished, lamely.

There was no time for lengthy recriminations so I had to accept his pathetic excuse and move on. 'There's no time for all that now,' I said. 'Even without your help I managed to smuggle Elvis into school. He's in Mr Timms' storeroom and I need your help to get him and take him into the science lesson.'

Kev was keen to make up for his earlier dismal performance and so, as the class headed off to the science labs, we trotted off to Mr Timms' store to fetch Elvis.

Now that the moment had arrived for Elvis to be presented, I felt quite elated. All the hassle had been worth it. The stick I'd got from Mum, the early morning start, the disappointment of Kev, Rob and Bill's non-arrival and the stress of the journey all now seemed events of a distant past as Kev and I wheeled Elvis proudly along the lower corridor of B Block towards Room B35, Mr Grimshaw's lab.

Needless to say, the appearance of a zebra in school (even a stuffed one) caused quite a stir, amongst the younger years especially. The corridor buzzed with excitement and they pointed, squealed and patted Elvis as we made our way past.

By the time we got to B35, the class had gone in but the door had not been closed. We could just hear Mr

Grimshaw inside saying, 'Right now, settle down everybody. Are we all here?'

As we nudged Elvis towards the door he continued, 'Good, if you could just get out your homework...'

Perfect timing or what!? Just as Mr Grimshaw asked for our homework, Elvis glided majestically into his line of sight, propelled from behind and still moving smoothly on his DIY roller blades.

Seldom are teachers lost for words. In fact, they are famous for being able to talk non-stop about nothing at all for hours on end, but Mr Grimshaw appeared to suffer complete loss of control over his vocal chords. As he and Elvis made eye contact, his mouth just fell open and stayed there.

The class all turned round to see what had stopped him so dead in his tracks, but the sight of Elvis that had rendered Mr Grimshaw incapable of speech or movement had completely the opposite effect on the members of 9H. Whereas Mr Grimshaw stood mute and still as a statue, all my classmates became hyperactive with excitement. As one they leapt from their lab stools, jostling for the best view of Elvis, and all speaking at the same time.

'Wow, look at that!', 'Where d'ya get it?', 'Nice one, Dave,' and so on.

To be honest, I was a little disappointed in Mr Grimshaw's reaction. I'd hoped for instant praise for my initiative in fulfilling the homework so completely, and his open-mouthed, trance-like state didn't quite confer the commendation that I felt I was due.

However, after a few minutes, the hubbub in the class died down and Mr Grimshaw began to regain the power of speech.

'What on *earth* do you think you are doing bringing that... that... monstrosity into my lesson? You stupid

boys! If this is your idea of a practical joke, I'm afraid I fail to see the funny side of it!'

It wasn't quite the response I'd been hoping for. He'd clearly misunderstood, so before he could continue with more in the same vein I cut in, 'No, sir, you don't understand...'

Mr Grimshaw was not yet in the mood for explanations. 'Oh I understand all right. I understand that two immature teenagers thought they'd get a laugh out of Mr Grimshaw by disrupting his lesson. That's it, isn't it?'

He glared angrily. He clearly had not understood, so I tried again to explain the situation.

'No, sir, honest. You've got it all wrong. This is my homework. I thought you'd be pleased with all the effort I've put in...'

'Your homework?' Mr Grimshaw sounded incredulous. He repeated himself, 'Your *homework*?'

'Yes, sir. You know, 'Take body horse-like mammal.' Kev told me, sir. Well, this is it. Elvis has got a body like a horse, hasn't he, sir?', and I smiled at Mr Grimshaw, trying to show him that far from causing him grief, I had wanted to brighten his Monday morning with my wholehearted completion of my homework.

His voice was amazed confusion as he echoed, '"Take body horse-like mammal"? What are you talking about? That wasn't your homework!'

'Well, it's what Kev had in his homework diary, sir,' I replied.

'Oh was it? Well, let's ask someone else what they have in *their* diary. Susan, let me see *your* homework diary,' he said, directing his command at Susan Smetherington-Smythe, who had never been known to make a mistake in her life.

He took the book which Susan offered and thumbed agitatedly to last Friday's date. 'Yes, here we are,' he read. '"Take Body course-work manual". I thought so. Your homework was simply to remember to bring in your Body course-work manual because we have finished our work on the human body and I want to collect in your folders before we move on to our next project.'

It was my turn to stand with my mouth open. I couldn't believe my ears. All this stress and hassle and Mr Grimshaw didn't want the body of a horse-like mammal at all. Despite the presence of the class and a still-simmering Mr Grimshaw, I turned on Kevin, who for the second time that morning had landed me in it.

'You stupid great lump of gunk. Now look what you've done. Why did you tell me that our homework was to bring a zebra to school when all we had to do was to remember our course-work manuals? You... you...'

Words failed me again as Kevin butted in, 'Well, I couldn't help it. You know what my writing's like and it *did* look like "take body horse-like mammal' in my book. If you hadn't forgotten to '

This time it was Mr Grimshaw's turn to interrupt but not, as you might expect, with the second chapter of his lecture. Instead, a deep throaty laugh started life some-where around his shoe-laces and erupted seconds later from his lips. Apparently now that he understood that Elvis' appearance in his room *had* been the result of a genuine mistake, he could see the funny side of the whole episode.

None of us could remember seeing a teacher laugh before. The unusual sight set off a chain reaction which soon saw the whole class, Kev and me included, rolling around in helpless fits of giggles. Every so often someone would regain enough composure to mutter 'body horse-like mammal' or 'zebra on skis', and off we'd all go again.

It was probably the best lesson we had all week (certainly Elvis seemed to enjoy himself), but then as I said, I always liked science lessons.

No, but seriously...

'It opened our eyes to previously unconsidered career possibilities...'

So what do you want to be when you leave school? Rocket scientist? Environmental protester? Or the person who puts those revolting green crunchy things inside Big Macs?

Whichever job you fancy, without doubt, it will be one of the biggest choices you make in the next few years.

For a few ideas about making well-wise career choices, turn to page 96.

On the other hand, if you're not really bothered, don't read on because the story just ended!

Choices, choices

The rest of this book will help you think through some of the issues that have arisen in the story about Elvis and me. Unlike Elvis, life's decisions are not always black and white, so if you are facing a big decision about friends or money or parents... or any of the things listed below, turn to the right page and read on...

HOW TO MAKE GOOD CHOICES

Many choices (like whether you choose to put your left sock on before your right one) are really not that important and you make them without even thinking. But some choices are more mega than that, so here's some help in making the sorts of choices that really matter.

CHOICES CHECK-UP

1 Choose right from wrong
When faced with a major choice, ask yourself, 'Is this an issue of "right and wrong"?' Some choices (like telling a lie) are *always* wrong and you should *always* avoid choosing 'wrong' rather than 'right'.

2 Choose what's best for others
Sometimes it's not quite so clear-cut, so how do you decide then? A good second question to ask is, 'Is anyone going to be hurt by this choice?' If they are, then maybe we should choose not to do it.

3 Choose what's in your best long-term interest
The next consideration is, 'Is it in my own best interests?' Beware of choosing to do things that might be fun at the time but later on leave you feeling guilty, or disappointed with yourself.

4 Choose what God wants
A big question if you are a Christian is, 'What does God think about this choice?' There may be specific help in the Bible or if you're still stuck, ask a Christian friend for advice. And don't forget to pray about it!

CHAPTER AND VERSE ON CHOOSING
Try to learn what pleases the Lord. Have nothing to do with the worthless things that people do ... be careful how you live (Ephesians 5:10,11,15, Good News Bible).

CHOOSING HOW TO GET ON WITH PARENTS

We don't choose our parents but the choices we make in our relationship with them are among the most important in our whole lives.

CHOICES CHECK-UP

1 Choose to communicate

Major problems arise in any relationship when people stop talking to one another. Take time to tell them (politely!) about what's bugging you, and find space to ask them to explain rules or decisions that you don't agree with.

2 Choose to forgive

When things go wrong (and they will), nothing is gained by bearing a grudge or acting sulkily. When you've calmed down, choose the right moment and either say 'Sorry' (if it's been your fault), or 'It's OK, let's forget it' (if it's been theirs).

3 Choose to understand

Worries about money, relationships or their work can leave parents burning on a short fuse. Maybe when they blow up at you, it's all the other things that are really stressing them out. It will help you if you choose to understand where their frustration is coming from.

4 Choose to respect

OK, they're not perfect, but your parents are probably doing their best. Show them a bit of respect, say 'Thanks' occasionally, help them out (before you're asked!) and listen to what they say – it's probably some of the best advice you'll get!

CHAPTER AND VERSE ON CHOOSING

It is your Christian duty to obey your parents, for this is the right thing to do. 'Respect your father and mother...'
(Ephesians 6:1,2, *Good News Bible*).

CHOOSING YOUR IMAGE

Choose carefully. Choose the right clothes, the right shoes, the right bike, even the right schoolbag, or people will reckon you're a geek. But are you really less of a person if you don't have the 'right' name on your trainers?

CHOICES CHECK-UP

1 Choose to be right inside first

The really important choices you make are about the sort of person you are on the inside. A spiteful person wearing Nikes is not going to be as popular as a thoughtful person wearing a store's own-brand.

2 Choose fashion that tells the truth about you

Most fashion comes with a built-in message: a short skirt or figure-hugging top says, 'I want you to look at my body'; a pierced nose or a shaved head might say, 'I'm a bit of a rebel'. Are your fashion choices telling the truth about you?

3 Choose creativity not conformity

Dress how you want to in order to express the person that you really are, and don't let other people squeeze you into their mould.

4 Choose an image you can afford!

Fashion is big business. The fashion industry doesn't care what you look like, they just want your money. Think about how much you can afford, shop around, check out charity shops and don't make yourself miserable by spending money you haven't got.

CHAPTER AND VERSE ON IMAGE

Don't copy the behaviour and customs of this world, but be a new and different person with a fresh newness in all you do and think (Romans 12:2, Living Bible).

CHOOSING YOUR FRIENDS

Some 'friends' are just class-mates who you hardly know, but other 'friends' are really close mates who you spend quite a bit of time with. Close friendships have a big influence on our lives; choose carefully!

CHOICES CHECK-UP

1 Choose friends who share your values

If your friends put you in a position where you are doing things that you later regret, have another think about whether they are the right friends for you.

2 Choose friends who are 'givers' and not just 'takers'

Good friends have the right to expect us to help them out, lend them things and be there for them. But people who only use you for what they can get out of you are not friends!

3 Choose some friends who share your faith

Try to make a good friendship with someone else who is a Christian. You can be a great source of strength and support for each other. And there are times when we all need a friend who will pray for us!

4 Choose to be a good friend yourself

Friendly people make friends most easily. Choose to be kind to others, be generous and reliable, and you'll have no trouble in making and keeping some really good friends.

CHAPTER AND VERSE ON CHOOSING FRIENDS

Keep company with the wise and you will become wise. If you make friends with stupid people, you will be ruined (Proverbs 13:20, *Good News Bible*).

CHOOSING HOW TO SPEND YOUR MONEY

The choices you make about spending are really important, because the way you cope with the little money you have now will determine how you cope with more later in life.

CHOICES CHECK-UP

1 Choose to think 'need' not 'want'
There will never be any shortage of things you *want*, but before buying something, ask yourself the question, 'Will my life go to pieces if I don't have this?' If the answer is 'yes', it's probably a need, if it's 'no' it's probably a want!

2 Choose to make up your own mind, not follow the crowd
Just because everyone else swallows the advertisers' hype and pays £80.00 for a pair of trainers, it doesn't mean that you have to! Spend your money on things that you think are important, and blow what anyone else thinks.

3 Choose to be generous
A good way to stop yourself getting too hooked on 'things' is to give away some of your money. Lend to a friend or give to charity; also try to give a proportion of what you get each week to your church as a way of thanking God for all that he has given you.

4 Choose to take God's wishes into account
The Bible teaches that all our money comes from God in the first place and is really only loaned to us; so think carefully about whether he is pleased with the way that you're spending his money!

CHAPTER AND VERSE ON MONEY CHOICES
Keep your lives free from the love of money, and be satisfied with what you have (Hebrews 13:5, *Good News Bible*).

CHOOSING WHO TO ASK OUT

The choices you make about boyfriend/girlfriend relationships are mega-important, partly because they can be so much more hurtful if they go wrong.

CHOICES CHECK-UP

1 Choose to wait
There is nothing wrong in choosing not to have a girlfriend or boyfriend. In the meantime, concentrate on building good friendships with your mates (male and female). Choose to wait until that 'special' friendship turns up.

2 Choose to keep other friendships alive
If you do start going out with someone, don't spend so much time with them that all your other friendships fall apart.

3 Choose not to go out with a non-Christian
If you are a Christian, it's not a good idea to start a close relationship with someone who doesn't share your faith.

4 Choose where to draw the line
All boyfriends and girlfriends hold hands, enjoy a cuddle, kiss and... Where do you stop? These four simple rules have helped a lot of couples choose to stop going too far:
- don't lie down together
- don't undress together
- don't explore under each other's clothing
- don't touch body parts which you haven't got yourself!

CHAPTER AND VERSE ON GOING OUT
*There is a right time for everything ... a time to hug; a time not to hug (*Ecclesiastes 3:1,5, *Living Bible).*

CHOOSING WHAT TO WATCH

Eat rubbish and you will damage your stomach; watch rubbish and you'll damage your mind. TV programmes, films, videos and Internet images that you watch need to be just as carefully monitored as your food intake.

CHOICES CHECK-UP

1 Choose to reject rubbish
Sometimes it's hard to tell when you start watching a programme what it's going to turn out like. Just because you've started watching something, it doesn't mean you have to finish watching it. If a good film turns into rubbish, hit the 'off' button or walk out of the cinema!

2 Choose to plan your viewing time
Don't be a couch slouch! Rather than just sitting in front of the box, flicking through the channels, try to get hold of a TV guide and plan ahead what you want to watch.

3 Choose to respect age guides
Films have age ratings for good reasons. Choose not to watch films at the cinema or on video at home until you are old enough. But remember that age ratings are only a guide and, even when you are officially old enough, not every film is worth watching.

4 Choose to view through God's eyes
While you're watching a programme, ask yourself if God is finding it good viewing.

CHAPTER AND VERSE ON WHAT TO WATCH
Fill your minds with those things that are good and that deserve praise: things that are true, noble, right, pure, lovely, and honourable (Philippians 4:8, Good News Bible).

CHOOSING HOW TO COPE WITH BROTHERS AND SISTERS

Brothers and sisters can be great friends one minute, and at each other's throats the next. If you have a brother or sister who sometimes drives you nuts, don't despair – you are not alone!

CHOICES CHECK-UP

1 Choose to be a fire extinguisher not a petrol pump!

When things start getting heated you can either walk away or you can argue back. If someone else is already smouldering, choose to damp things down rather than add fuel to their fire.

2 Choose to be yourself, let others be themselves

Give your brother or sister space to be themselves. Don't feel cross if your parents treat you differently: they have to because you *are* different individuals. Remember, being treated differently is not the same as being treated unfairly.

3 Choose to be positive

You will get a lot more out of any relationship if you show an interest in the other person, act kindly towards them and encourage them. Try it; it even works with brothers and sisters!

4 Choose to count to ten

Avoid getting drawn in to name-calling and exchanging insults. If you do say something that you later regret, go back and say sorry. Don't let bad feeling drag on for days.

CHAPTER AND VERSE ON BROTHERS AND SISTERS

Don't pick on people, jump on their failures, criticise their faults unless, of course, you want the same treatment (Matthew 7:1, The Message).

CHOOSING A GOOD CHURCH

Churches come in all styles, shapes and sizes. No one church has got it all right, and none has got it all wrong, so you are free to choose the best church for you. Here are some guidelines:

CHOICES CHECK-UP

1 Choose a church where they act as if Jesus is alive

Church isn't supposed to be a monument to a dead God, but a family where a living God still talks to his people and helps them in their lives.

2 Choose a church where the Bible is taken seriously

God has given us the Bible to help us stay on course in our relationship with him. The less the Bible is used, the more likely it is that a church will go off course!

3 Choose a church where young people can get involved

There is no age limit to being useful at church. God doesn't want you to wait until you're eighteen before you can get involved, so find a church where you can use your gifts now.

4 Choose a church and stick with it

No church is perfect and if you keep changing from one to another every time someone upsets you, you will lose out in the end. Once you have made your choice, get involved and be loyal to your church and its leaders through the ups and the downs.

CHAPTER AND VERSE ON CHURCH

Let's see how inventive we can be in encouraging love and helping out, not avoiding worshipping together as some do but spurring each other on... (Hebrews 10:25, *The Message*).

CHOOSING TO TELL THE TRUTH

We all get into situations where it would be a lot less hassle to lie rather than tell the truth. But telling lies nearly always gets us into hotter water eventually and anyway, whether we get found out or not, it's wrong!

CHOICES CHECK-UP

1 Choose to tell the truth to others
No one can make you tell a lie, it is entirely your choice. Make a decision now to tell the truth in every circumstance, and don't allow yourself to believe for one minute that telling a lie is no big deal.

2 Choose to tell the truth, kindly
Sometimes you will need to think *how* to tell the truth. Pointing out someone's faults in a very blunt way may be 'telling them the truth' but it may not be the kindest way to do it.

3 Choose to tell the truth to yourself
The most common lies we tell ourselves concern undervaluing ourselves ('I'm no good at anything'), or overvaluing ourselves ('I'm just so perfect!'). Choose to look honestly at yourself and you will find that the truth is not at either extreme.

4 Choose to make the right choices!
Telling lies is a way of getting ourselves out of trouble. The best way to eliminate the need to lie is to avoid doing something wrong in the first place.

CHAPTER AND VERSE ON TELLING LIES
Stop lying to each other; tell the truth, for we are parts of each other and when we lie to each other we are hurting ourselves (Ephesians 4:25, Living Bible).

CHOOSING WHAT TO DO WHEN
PEOPLE LET YOU DOWN

People sometimes hurt us or let us down. It happens all the time, so the question is not, 'How can we stop people hurting us?', but 'How do we choose to respond when they do?'

CHOICES CHECK-UP

1 Choose to forgive
The only real choice is to forgive someone who wrongs us. Any other way of responding (for example, by hurting them back, or by harbouring bitterness towards them) only ends up making things worse.

2 Choose to forgive first
Don't wait for the other person to make the first move but be the first to say, 'It's OK, let's forget it.' Don't damage yourself by carrying around a load of anger and bitterness.

3 Choose to minimise the hurt
If someone is *always* letting you down, then they need to be made aware of how their behaviour makes you feel. If a friend always returns your bike with a puncture, it is not unreasonable to say, 'If you don't fix it before you return it, it won't be available again.'

4 Choose to get some advice
If someone is hurting you big-time, then you probably need to get some help from another person. Simply forgiving someone who is bullying you or abusing you isn't the best way to help that person learn how to be different. In cases like that, get outside help.

CHAPTER AND VERSE ON FORGIVING
Forgive one another as quickly and thoroughly as God in Christ forgave you (Ephesians 4:32, The Message).

CHOOSING JUST THE JOB

Maybe you are getting close to making option choices at school. Those choices will affect the sort of job that you might end up doing so here are a few things to help you in making this mammoth choice.

CHOICES CHECK-UP

1 Choose a job that you think you will enjoy
A job that you will enjoy is probably going to be better for you than a job which pays loads of money but which you hate.

2 Consider choosing a job that helps others
The most satisfying jobs are those where you feel that you are really helping other people and getting paid for it! There are all sorts of jobs that make life better for others, so think how your interests and skills could help other people.

3 Choose a job that uses the gifts God has given you
God is interested in the job choices you make. He has given you certain gifts and a certain personality. Try to choose a job which makes sense of the person God has made you.

4 Ask an older Christian what they think you should choose
In all probability, your careers guidance at school will not be given by a Christian. Listen carefully to the help you get from school, but check out your ideas with another Christian to get an idea of what God thinks of the choices you are making.

CHAPTER AND VERSE ON CHOOSING A JOB
Whatever you do, work at it with all your heart, as though you were working for the Lord and not for human beings (Colossians 3:23, *Good News Bible*).